Twelve Steps Through The Bible

GOD'S WAY OF RECOVERY FROM ADDICTION FOR PEOPLE OF FAITH

Don Wilkerson

Copyright © 2024 by Don Wilkerson

ISBN 9798880062195

Unless otherwise noted, all Scriptures are taken from the New King James Version®. Copyright © 1982 by Thomas Nelson. Used by permission. All rights reserved.

Scripture quotations marked CEV are from the Contemporary English Version Copyright © 1991, 1992, 1995 by American Bible Society. Used by Permission.

Scripture quotations marked MSG are taken from The Message, copyright © 1993, 2002, 2018 by Eugene H. Peterson. Used by permission of NavPress. All rights reserved. Represented by Tyndale House Publishers.

Scripture quotations marked NLT are taken from the Holy Bible, New Living Translation, copyright ©1996, 2004, 2015 by Tyndale House Foundation. Used by permission of Tyndale House Publishers, Carol Stream, Illinois 60188. All rights reserved.

Scripture quotations marked NIV are taken from The Holy Bible, New International Version ®, NIV ®. Copyright © 1973, 1978, 1984, 2011 by Biblica, Inc.® Used by permission. All rights reserved worldwide.

Scripture quotations marked MSG are taken from THE MESSAGE. Copyright © 1993, 2002, 2018 by Eugene H. Peterson. Used by permission of NavPress. All rights reserved. Represented by Tyndale House Publishers, a Division of Tyndale House Ministries.

TPT: Scripture quotations marked TPT are taken from The Passion Translation®. Copyright © 2017, 2018 by Passion & Fire Ministries, Inc. Used by permission. All rights reserved. ThePassionTranslation.com.

Scripture quotations marked KJV are taken from the King James Version.

CONTENTS

Introduction	5
The Twelve Steps	11
1. ADMIT... POWERLESS	13
2. RESTORE... SANITY	25
3. DECISION... TURN OVER	34
4. SEARCHING... INVENTORY	48
5. ADMITTED... WRONGS	58
6. DEFECTS... OF CHARACTER	70
7. REMOVE... SHORTCOMINGS	79
8. MAKE... AMENDS	88
9. AMENDS... TO [SPECIFIC] PEOPLE	99
10. CONTINUE... INVENTORY	110
11. PRAYING... FOR HIS WILL	123
12. CARRY... THIS MESSAGE	134
Other Recommended Resource Material	146
About the Author	148

ACKNOWLEDGEMENTS

I would like to thank my wife Cindy for being patient and understanding towards me as I write my books. There are times when she says something to me and it goes in one ear and out the other. I make excuses, saying, "Sorry Honey, but I'm in a zone!" By that I mean I feel so inspired and so focused on what I'm writing that I don't hear (or want to hear) anything that might distract me. Of course, a wife should never be considered "a distraction!"

A thank you to Charles Simpson, a longtime friend and former Prayer Pastor with my brother and I at Times Square Church (and later also Prayer Pastor, mentor, and counselor at Brooklyn Teen Challenge). He now pastors a church in Queens, New York. He has edited this book and has helped me on many of my writing projects for which I am grateful. Without his help, this book would not have happened.

A word of appreciation to Ray Rosa (Executive Director of The Dominican Republic Teen Challenge) for writing the feedback sections of each chapter. Ray is well qualified to make comments on each of the 12 Steps as he came out of a life of deep addiction and by the grace of God found freedom in Christ at Long Island Teen Challenge. Though Ray never went through A.A. or any other 12 Step Program, he shares on how each of the 12 Steps as written in this book helped him to understand the need for a Higher Power in overcoming addiction which he found in Jesus Christ.

INTRODUCTION

The famous—and at times, highly successful—12 Steps from the Alcoholics Anonymous programs are highlighted in the following 12 chapters, examining Biblical examples of individuals whose "God-connections" illustrate the message of each Step. These 12 Steps are designed for those who desire sobriety and freedom from addiction to alcoholism, opioids, and other life-controlling substances. (I will be using the Twelve Steps for Christians from the book of the same title, published by RPI Publishers. That list is found on pages 11-12.)

As we study men and women in the Bible who found hope and healing, we can see the message and power of each of these Steps. For example, in Second Samuel, King David committed a terrible sin. His lust for Bathsheba may or may not have been the result of a life-controlling problem of lust, but the way he dealt with it at first (denial, and then confession), clearly illustrates the message of Step 5.

In the New Testament book of Acts, Chapter 3, we find a man who was a powerless cripple, unable to manage his life. He is an example of Step 1, which says, "We admitted we were powerless over the effects of our separation from God—that our lives had become unmanageable."

These 12 Steps originated in Alcoholics Anonymous to help alcoholics find a spiritual pathway to freedom from their life-controlling problem. These Steps have biblical teachings at their roots, as we will see when we examine each one. Thus, the reason for this book.

Those who teach them can take these Steps lightly, along with those who endeavor to follow them. Each Step can be taught with a strong evangelical emphasis, or they can be received as general principles to follow, almost in a secular way. For example, Step 3 talks about "God as we understood Him." That can mean something quite different to various people. I'm advocating here that when the 12 Steps are followed and taught with a strong biblical emphasis, they will prove much more successful than when used in just a general way. One can lightly tip toe through the Steps or go through them by stepping firming on the biblical truths associated with each, desiring to fully embrace them.

Defining a "Higher Power" can be having either faith in God through Jesus Christ or some nebulous belief in a lesser power than our Creator God. One can be an atheist or agnostic and still work through the 12 Steps. Another way of

INTRODUCTION

stating different ways the Steps can be interpreted is either liberal or conservative, either as principles with no biblical connection, or as truths found in the Bible.

Twelve Steps Through the Bible is a book in which the "Steps" are not considered light Steps, but ones firmly rooted in the Scriptures. I have known many who did the 12 Steps in A.A., and as a result, have lived years clean and sober. In many cases, they also became born-again Christians. I would meet them from time to time in churches where I was speaking. Church-based 12 Step Recovery Ministries, in my estimation, have the greatest success working with alcoholics and drug addicts. Of course, there are many participants who do not experience the new life in Christ, yet they still benefit from following the Steps and are enjoying a lifetime of recovery. We might say they benefited from the principles of the Scriptures while not following Christ.

At one time, I was negative towards those who completed the 12 Steps of A.A., mainly because of what I thought it was not. Not biblical enough! Not evangelistic enough! And because Jesus was often left out of the Steps. Then, when I saw how many people were helped by attending A.A. meetings, I saw this for what it was and is—Steps to recovery. It can eventually (hopefully) lead anyone who applies these Steps to a relationship with God in Christ. It does not lead every user to such an encounter, but it can; and it often depends on who sponsors the group meeting. Biblical based churches that sponsor the 12 Steps to Recovery are best equipped to apply these Steps to the truths found in the Bible.

I also found it hard at first to accept A.A. participants who said they were sober, yet they claimed to still be an alcoholic. Eventually, I came to accept that if someone felt being a sober "alcoholic" motivated them to abstain "one day at a time" from drinking, who was I to criticize that. I now do not. Still, I believe there are in the 12 Steps signposts that can lead one to a personal encounter with God through Jesus Christ where we become new creations, and the old has passed away.

The wise men who came from the East did not travel westward in order to find the town of Bethlehem. All they were doing was following the star. It led them to a Star in Bethlehem called in Revelation 22:16, "The Bright and Morning Star." They knew the star was significant, so when they found the child Jesus, they worshipped Him. Sadly, others come close to knowing and worshiping Jesus, but do not. I would prefer everyone who does the 12 Steps of A.A. to

INTRODUCTION

become a born-again Christian, but it's their choice to do so or not. Even if not, it is better to be sober than a habitual drinker; or worse, a drunk.

This book is divided into 12 chapters, one for each of the Twelve Steps. The title of each chapter is from one or more words from the Twelve Steps. These words are then highlighted from Scriptures based upon those words. In this way, the 12 Steps are then *Twelve Steps Through the Bible*. I'm writing this book with certain assumptions. They are:

1. You believe the Bible is God's truth for your life.
2. You want to experience a new life and be set free from your life-controlling problem.
3. You believe God is manifest in His Son, Jesus.
4. The mention of God within the 12 Steps is also the same as Jesus.
5. You are or desire to be born again by a spiritual and supernatural rebirth.
6. You identify the Higher Power as being the living God revealed through His Son, the Jesus of the Bible.

This book is also designed and written for faith-based ministries and churches to use in small group settings, applying the 12 Steps of A.A. in their outreach to addicts and alcoholics. If such rehab ministries and churches do not yet use the 12 Step Program, this book may give them a reason to do so.

Don Wilkerson

THE TWELVE STEPS

Slightly modified, cited in *The Twelve Steps for Christians*[1] For the Original A.A. 12 Steps, go to **https://al-anon.org/ for-members/the-legacies/the-twelve-steps/**

STEP ONE: We admitted we were powerless over the effects of our separation from God—that our lives had become unmanageable.

STEP TWO: Came to believe that a power greater than ourselves could restore us to sanity.

STEP THREE: Made a decision to turn our will and our lives over to the care of God as we understood Him.

STEP FOUR: Made a searching and fearless moral inventory of ourselves.

STEP FIVE: Admitted to God, to ourselves, and to another human being the exact nature of our wrongs.

STEP SIX: Were entirely ready to have God remove all these defects of character.

STEP SEVEN: Humbly asked Him to remove our shortcomings.

STEP EIGHT: Made a list of all persons we had harmed and became willing to make amends to them all.

STEP NINE: Made direct amends to such people wherever possible, except when to do so would injure them or others.

STEP TEN: Continued to take personal inventory, and when we were wrong, promptly admitted it.

STEP ELEVEN: Sought through prayer and meditation to improve our conscious contact with God as we understood Him, praying only for knowledge of His will for us and the power to carry that out.

STEP TWELVE: Having had a spiritual awakening as the result of these steps, we tried to carry this message to others, and to practice these principles in all our affairs.

1

ADMIT... POWERLESS

STEP 1: We *admitted* we were *powerless* over the effects of our separation from God—that our lives had become unmanageable.

And I know that nothing good lives in me, that is, in my sinful nature. I want to do what is right, but I can't. (Romans 7:18 NLT)

If you are ready to call it quits—from a past and a present that is destroying both the present and future of your life, then join "The Sobriety Club." There is one and only one qualification for joining this remarkable group: to be willing to take Step One by "admitting" and submitting to a new way of thinking, taking "one step at a time" and "one day at a time." Once finishing the journey of these Steps, you will be a lifetime member of "The Sobriety Club," living out sanity, serenity, and salvation! If you want to know the meaning of hope, healing, health, and happiness, then decide right now to Step into the future.

As shared above, as we go through each of the A.A. Steps, this journey will also take us through the Bible. We will examine Bible characters who teach something of each Step by understanding the characteristics and examples of these individuals. Another way this can be described is taking the traditional 12 Steps and baptizing them in the Word and the Spirit to see their biblical roots.

We begin with a man whose name we do not know, but whose story of healing is truly a miraculous encounter with Jesus Christ. He went from laying at the gate of the temple in Jerusalem to running and leaping in that same temple. In the third chapter of the book of Acts, the Apostles Peter and John were going into the temple at an appointed hour of prayer. On the way in, a beggar caught their attention. He had been crippled—powerless—for 38 long years. He just wanted a few coins to live on. Acts 3:1-3 states,

> Now Peter and John went up together to the temple at the hour of prayer, the ninth hour. And a certain man lame from his mother's womb was carried, whom they laid daily at the temple which is called Beautiful, to ask alms from those who entered the temple.

There are physical cripples and moral and spiritual ones, as well. Alcohol and drug addiction renders the user powerless to manage their lives as other free people. They do not have the power to make wise decisions. Their will is captivated by their desire to feed themselves on their substance of choice.

The difference between physical cripples and those crippled by their addiction is that the former have no choice in their inability to rightly function in society. However, those crippled by their drug of choice can choose to be set free from their life-controlling problem by making a new and better choice—the choice to be set free. This begins by an admission of their problem. The Bible's word for "admit" is "confession." And Who should this confession be confessed to? "We *admitted* we were *powerless* over the effects of our separation from God." Right from the start, the 12 Steps recognize that it is God that one must turn to for help and forgiveness.

It's true, addiction separates the addict from family, loved ones, friends, and society; but first and foremost there is alienation from God. There is no getting away from finding sanity and sobriety without going to and before God.

This encounter between the Apostle Peter and John

with a crippled beggar portrays what it's like to go through life enslaved to a poisonous substance:

1. The cripples (whether physically, morally or spiritually) are "carried" through life because they are powerless to function on their own.

Acts 3:2 says, "And a certain man lame from his mother's womb was carried..." When separated from God, you will always be an outsider. The temple represents the place of worship and connection to the Higher Power. This man was at the gate of the temple. His condition did not allow him to go inside the temple—to worship. Jesus said, "I am the gate; whoever enters through me will be saved." (John 10:9 NIV) Addiction and sin keeps you outside that door—outside the gate that leads to a new life.

2. When you can't manage your own life, you need something or someone other than your own will and power to exist.

Drugs and alcohol are what carries the addict through life:

"Whom they laid daily at the gate of the temple." As long as this man stayed in his physical condition, he could not participate in the normal activities of life. So it is with the psychological, spiritual, and even physical cravings that immobilize the addicted drinker and drug user. "Normal" is for everyone else; not for them. We might even say addicts are on a life-support system in which they merely exist, but not fully live.

In addiction, the user's emotions and spiritual life are numbed, frozen, and leaves the person as if unconscious to the possibility of wholesome pleasures, peace, and living a truly purpose-driven life. It is not different from being a prisoner who loses life's freedoms. The drink or drug of choice becomes, as it were, a god that demands dedication to none else or nothing else but that god.

3. What was the cause of this man's crippled condition?

We can say that he had no choice about being crippled, for he was born with such a handicap. However, in the Jewish culture and religion of that day, they attributed all physical ailments either to the sin of that individual or his or her parents (See John 9:2). There is an analogy in this to addiction. The Bible says, "All have sinned and come short of the glory of God."(Romans 3:23) Addicts and alcoholics are not sinners because they are users; they are users because they are first sinners, as we all are.

The key to recovery is acknowledging our inbred sin. As this man was born crippled, so the Bible says, "Behold, I was shapen in iniquity, and in sin did my mother conceive me." (Psalm 51:5 KJV) Is that fair? Many do not think it is, and reject the premise of being born a sinner, but it's hard to prove otherwise. Perfection does not exist in the human race. Sin does.

One way some have chosen to deal with their defects and wrongs committed that the Bible simply calls "sin" is to take a trip to LaLa Land. An addict is not a sinner because they are addicted, but they are addicted because they are, first of all, a sinner. The crippled man was a sinner regardless of his addiction, and through his healing, he was given new legs. But, more importantly, he was given a new heart and a new life. This is why the first thing he did was to enter the temple leaping and praising God.

4. Note the shame and unmanaged life of this man.

Peter said, "Look on us." (Acts 3:4) This man could not look others in the eye. Shame will do that to you. You may think this man had no reason to feel ashamed since he was not to be blamed for his condition. But he was in that culture and time, as pointed out above. This man carried double shame: the shame of his crippled condition and the shame of being a beggar.

> At times of greatest shame, we need to do the exact opposite of what we feel like doing. We need to lift our faces to our God, open our mouths in confession, and let Him wash us with forgiveness and bathe us with radiance.[2] (Beth Moore)

Addiction renders the user powerless to function as a normal person, and that will always result in shame.

5. The man had false expectations.

"So he gave them [Peter and John] his attention, expecting to receive something from them." (Acts 3:8) The addict is used to having hopes dashed when and if seeking help. They are told they have a disease that will never go away. This guarantees that the help providers will always have clients—the same ones over and over again. How true in this case is the Scripture from Proverbs 23:7 that says, "For as a man thinketh in his heart, so is he." (KJV) In A.A. this is sometimes called "stinking thinking."

6. The crippled do not need coins. They need a cure.

They don't need a Band-Aid. They need healing. They don't need treatment. They need to be recovered, not just *recovery*. What the fake peddlers cannot do for the addicted cripples, a preacher can do: proclaim the truth of Acts 3:6:

> Then Peter said, "Silver and gold I do not have, but what I do have I give you: in the name of Jesus Christ of Nazareth rise up and walk."

The addiction problem is not solved with money. Addiction treatment, medical wise, is a business without cures. What I like about A.A. and 12 Step groups is that it is done at little or no cost. Peter did not say, "Wise up and walk, pay up and walk, medicate up and walk, and accept you have a disease you just need to live with." Peter said, "Rise up and walk" because Jesus got up and walked out of the grave and He entrusted His disciples to use His name to heal the sick, the cripples, and even raise the dead, spiritually and physically. 1 Corinthians 6:14 says, "God both raised up the Lord and will also raise us up by His power."

> Because of the resurrection, everything changes. Death changes. It used to be the end; now it is the beginning.[3] (Max Lucado)

This is true regarding physical death; but also in respect to death from sin—we are raised to new life in Christ.

FOLLOW-UP REFLECTIONS ON STEP 1

1. Suppose you got into a car to drive it, and it would only go about 15 miles an hour, then slowly lose all power. Have you come to the point where you know you have lost power and control over your life? If so, how and why?

2. Have you considered that your need of the 12 Steps is because of the effects of having lost contact with God? If so, explain.

3. Has God been a part of your life up to now? Explain.

4. List 3 ways your life is unmanageable now.

5. In the crippled man's situation (begging outside the temple), how do you see this as a reflection of your life now?

FEEDBACK FROM A PARTICIPANT OF STEP 1

I translate the word "admitted" in the 12 Steps to "repentance," which is the first Step to acknowledging and confessing one's sins to God. This involved recognizing that I have done wrong, taking responsibility for my actions, and expressing sincere remorse and regret for them. This first Step is the cornerstone or foundation upon which all other healing (Steps) can take place. I quickly realized that the "outside" help wasn't what I really needed. I needed "inside" help. This was the help I soon came to understand in the form of salvation and healing through Christ. It wasn't that something externally needed to change, it was that something internally needed to be healed. —Ray Rosa

A PRAYER TO PRAY

"Lord, help me to rise up and walk straight, strong, and secure by Your grace and power, just like what You did for the crippled man. I don't want any longer to be what I was, but to embrace a new future that You promise is available for me—yes, even me. I want to break from the thought patterns and behaviors that made me fall into a lifestyle of bondage.

Reveal the lies that caused me to fall, and replace them with Your truth so I can think and live differently. Thank You!"

A BIBLE PROMISE TO CLAIM

For when the time was right, the Anointed One came and died to demonstrate his love for sinners who were entirely helpless, weak, and powerless to save themselves.

(Romans 5:6 The Passion Translation)

2
RESTORE... SANITY

STEP 2: Came to believe a Power greater than ourselves could *restore* us to *sanity*.

God is working in you, giving you the desire and power to do what pleases Him. (Philippians 2:13 NLT)

> Christianity if false, is of no importance and, if true, is of infinite importance. The one thing it cannot be is moderately important.[4] (C.S. Lewis)

What powerful words these are in Step Two, beginning with "believe." The God Connection needs a drug or alcohol 're-connection' in and with a small group of seekers in a 12 Step process, replacing sitting in a bar or connecting with a drug supplier.

Someone might say, "But I find it hard to believe in this Greater Power."

Wait just a minute. If you are taking some type of drug, you must have faith that it's not going to kill you. If you drink every day, you are committing suicide "one day at a time" and one drink at a time. It's called *death on the installment plan.*

You can "come to believe" if you want to believe. Belief and faith needs boosters. A booster is when you are in an environment where those around you are drinking in the water of life such as when Jesus gave the Samaritan woman "living water." (Read John chapter 4) Being involved in church life will help turn weak faith into believing faith. "Church life" should be more than attending church, but developing new relationships, possible new friends and even the possibility of a mentor.

Note Step 2 says, "Come to believe." This indicates that believing is a process—a spiritual journey. If you were raised in a home where Christianity was like some foreign religion and you never gave serious thought about God or the life and teachings of Christ, then believing may be hard for you. Belief and faith are necessary to connect with the Power to restore you to wholeness and new thought patterns such as being *restored to sanity.* Just because someone does not believe does not mean it does not exist.

God wants to be wanted. He does not invade your space unless you let Him. Faith is *the key that unlocks the door* to a changed life. Faith can connect you to the "Greater

Power" rather than the destructive power in a powder, a pill, a weed, a bag of heroin or cocaine or other drugs of choice.

Addiction is a prison to the soul. Someone has described addicts as "hollow men and women" whose lives have no meaning and purpose; it is a life that separates us from the Higher Power that is the wellspring of life. Until we include the spiritual aspect of life, our souls will be empty and hungry. A woman of faith found healing from a blood issue and is a good example of someone was made whole by her simple touch of Jesus' garment. She is simply referred to by as a woman with "an issue of blood." (Matthew 9:20 KJV)

The woman with determination pushed through a crowd surrounding Jesus for she had said to herself, "If only I may touch His garment, I shall be healed." (Matthew 9:21) How did she know or believe this? Either because she heard of the specific healings other experienced or she had followed Jesus from a distance, and then one day found He was on the same road or path she was on.

How then is she a person that typifies addiction and one who seeks and finds the answer?

1. **She tried unsuccessfully other remedies for her condition:** "She had suffered a great deal under

the care of many doctors… yet instead of getting better, she grew worse." (Mark 5:26 NIV)

2. **The good thing is that she did not give up hope and in spite of finding no answer to her "issue" she kept searching.**

3. **She was desperate for help and when she knew the One who had the power to heal was within reach, she seized the moment.**

4. **She turned an "if only" as an act of faith:** "If only I may touch His clothes, I shall be made whole." (Mark 5:28)

5. **She had a blood disease and so do addicts who inject their bloodstream with what causes a euphoria, but over time does harm to the body, mind, and soul.**

Step 2 requires the kind of thinking and action of this woman. She didn't say she hoped she would be healed. She didn't say, "If it's God's will, I will be healed." She didn't leave her "If" as a question unanswered, but said just a touch of Jesus and "I shall be healed." This is faith in a "greater Power than" herself.

The lesson from her is: *reach and be restored.* Believe and be restored to sanity. You may come from a faith tradition in which, because of your past, you thought God either ignored you, punished you, or will make you do some kind of penance. An unhealthy fear of God can compound your guilt and shame. All He wants is, like with this woman, your desire to reach Him, your faith that He will answer your need, and your humility in coming to Him. This woman didn't expect special treatment. She touched his hem, bending down to do so. Martin Luther said, "He that can humble himself earnestly before God in Christ, has already won."

Another thing we learn from the healing of this woman with a blood disease: she was not the one Jesus was on the way to help. She was not the first choice to be helped, but Jesus was *her* first choice to be the One she reached out to be healed. As Jesus was on His way to minister to the daughter of Jairus the leader of the local synagogue (Mark 5: 21-24; 5: 35-43), this woman stopped Jesus in His tracks. That is what faith will do.

If you think Jesus is not for you to be the One to change your life, then do what this woman did: get His attention. Ask! Have faith, even if at first, you have doubts! I wrote in my *Challenge Study Bible* on this:

> There are many ways for a woman today to see herself in this woman: lost in a crowd, feeling rejected by society, labeled an outcast. But she was determined to find a cure simply by touching Jesus. Are you that person now who needs to touch Jesus for healing or for life transformation? Ignore the crowds, press through your fears, and present yourself to Jesus. His power can flow out of Him into you. (Luke 8:43)[5]

FOLLOW UP REFLECTIONS ON STEP 2

1. Explain how you came to believe you needed a power greater than yourself to be ready to receive help?

2. What has been your concept of God?

3. What would being restored to sanity be like for you?

4. On a scale of one to ten regarding the strength or weakness of your faith now (with one being almost none and ten having a strong faith) what would your number be? Explain the reason for the number you listed?

5. Does this woman's contact with Jesus describe how you want Him to respond to your situation?

FEEDBACK FROM A PARTICIANT OF STEP 2

After having visited doctors and psychologists for many years and even hearing people like teachers always saying that my condition was incurable, I realized that if they couldn't help, then there was only one choice for me to get help. It was obvious that I needed God more than ever. Only He could heal me... I was referred to a place by my pastor called Teen Challenge. When I got there, my prayers were answered! I knew in my heart only God could heal me... if I gave Him a chance. My first step to healing was surrendering to Him my heart, desires and will. I had to acknowledge that I was helpless. I had to surrender. That first step of surrender came through the form of accepting Christ as my Lord and Savior. I was no longer at war with Him. I was no longer opposed to Him, no longer His enemy. I obtained what is called peace with God. I signed an unconditional truce. —Ray Rosa

A PRAYER TO PRAY

"Heavenly Father, thank You for making it possible to know You. I do believe You are the One, and the only One Higher Power that can restore me to having a sound mind. Please remove my thought patterns of the past that led me downward to destruction because of my addictive behavior. I need Your total cure of my total person by the power of Your Holy Spirit."

A PROMISE TO CLAIM

I'm asking you now to keep following the instructions as though I were right there with you...
God will continually revitalize you, implanting within you the passion to do what pleases him.

(Philippians 2:12-13 The Passion Translation)

3
DECISION... TURN OVER

STEP 3: Made a *decision* to *turn* our will and our lives *over* to the care of God as we understood Him.

Teach me to do Your will, for You are my God. Your Spirit is good; lead me to the land of uprightness. (Psalm 143:10)

> Even if you've missed God's plan entirely for years and years, His plan can still swing into operation the minute you're ready to step up and step in, with God at your side.[6] (Tony Evans)

This Step 3 is a critical point in the journey to wholeness and sobriety. Many people live by "I won't" but God's desire is an "I will." The decision to "turn our will over" to something and Someone else is a struggle between one's will being captive to a power they seem unable to turn away from to a new way of life. The question is which *power* is going to win out—the power of drugs and or alcohol or the power of God? God never forces Himself on anyone. He comes only by invitation. Everyone comes to God by a decision of their will, and not just those working the 12 Steps.

In my early days of working with addicts at a time when there was a much greater stigma to addiction than now, and when there were not the rehab and detox places as there are now, many addicts tried on their own, by their sheer will power to kick the habit or "get the monkey off their back" as they referred to getting clean and sober. I'd invite addicts to come into our faith-based residential program and they'd say, "Reverend, I have to do this on my own will power." I would respond and say, "Your right and your wrong. It takes your will but it takes a Higher Power then your own power." Then I'd add, "If you have the *will*—God has the *power*." Those two things together will help you overcome your addiction. God and His power and your will is a powerful combination—it can beat all addiction.

Will Power is the power to surrender to *The Higher Power of all Higher Powers* found in God through Jesus Christ. As I said, God only comes by invitation. He says, "I stand at the door and knock." (Revelation 3:20) He won't bust through the door. But He will send His Holy Spirit to convict and convince you to make the decision to open the door of your heart and allow God to take up residence inside you. Apart from the Holy Spirit, the greatest power you have need for in your life is the power to choose. God has given you the power to choose—now is time to make new and right choices.

This choice can be between the power to choose life or death; between being clean or staying unclean; between being at peace or being at war with yourself. Why would you want to choose to be under a power that keeps you from being the person God chose you to be from your birth? God does not make junk—the devil does. You were not destined to be a loser. God's will is for you to succeed in life. When your will is surrendered to His will, He remakes you into "a new creation." (See 2 Corinthians 5:17)

> Every person, in coming to the knowledge of himself, is not only urged to seek God, by also [are led by] the Hand to find Him.[7] (John Calvin)

Step 3 ends by saying, "made a decision to turn our will and our lives over to God as we understood Him." Note the word is not "understand" but "understood" Him, past tense. This is important. You may have not understood God, for example, as a child as if the Bible was like a fairytale. A nice story, but then you grew out of it and God was alienated in your life. You may have kept Him at a distance or as nonexistent.

Maybe you misunderstood God because you were in a church that had a rule-based message of how to know God: do this, do not do that. So you gave up on the church and in doing so, you gave up on God. Or, you may have been in a church or religious tradition by which you were led to believe God loves you no matter what you do. On one extreme are those who live by a rule-based faith, and on the other end are those who live by a no-rules at all faith.

Another way you may have an understanding of God is that He loves you just as you are, so you end up doing as you please because God is good and He understands you have a disease and you have to live with your addiction. All these ideals might be described as the baggage you carry when you desire to come to God.

How then can you come to God in the way in which He desires for you to understand Him? The answer is in the Big Book, the Bible. The Bible is God's personal message to us. The 12 Steps without the Bible is like having a map, but never riding in a car. The Bible takes you somewhere. Its message shows you how to live free, sober, clean, successful, and sane.

The sad truth is that many who attend A.A. meetings don't read the Bible. They learn how to admit wrongs, but unless also learning how to be right and live right, the Steps are like being on a merry-go-round.

I have always said that the good thing about A.A. are the group meetings. The bad thing about A.A. are the group meetings. I heard about a doctor that often went to 3 A.A. meetings a day and he said in one year he went to over 400 meetings. He was sober and I have to give him credit for that. But he was overly dependent on this group encounter. There is a better way. The 12 Steps are not an end in and of themselves. What about Step 13 and going forward. I could name about 25 and more Steps I have taken in my spiritual journey.

Let me now use as an example in Step 3 of a young man whose grandfather was a king and his father was David's best friend Jonathan. His name was Mephibosheth. Though he was born in a palace, he lived for years in obscurity—a place called Lo-Debar that means "without pasture" which we can take to mean a desert-like environment. This grandson of King Saul experienced two tragedies in his life: at age five he, with his nurse, fled the King's palace when it was under attack. He fell and became permanently lame. When his father Jonathan and grandfather Saul were killed in the civil war between David's army and Saul's army, that is when Mephibosheth went to live in exile.

I chose Mephibosheth as someone much like those that are sincere seekers after sobriety in A.A., Celebrate Recovery, or other similar groups. Here is why "Mo," as I nickname him fits the 12 Step profile for the following reasons:

1. He was born into the upper class.

Addiction is no respecter of race, religion, or class. My experience in ministry to addicts goes back to the 1960's when most people I worked with were from the inner city. They were hardcore addicts. Then I became a co-pastor in a church. Following that, I launched an overseas ministry for addicts. Then in 2008, I returned to Brooklyn to lead the original Teen Challenge my brother David and I co-founded. The drug scene had changed drastically by then and in addition to the hardcore heroin and cocaine addicts, a new class were caught up in the opioid epidemic. As such, I began working with college grads and dropouts, professional and career dropout workers, and those who grew up in many faith and church traditions. Mephibosheth came from royalty, but to no fault of his own, lost it all.

2. Mephibosheth came from a life of shame.

Here is the account of the tragedy in Mephibosheth's life:

> Jonathan, Saul's son, had a son who was lame in his feet. He was five years old when the news about Saul and Jonathan came from Jezreel, and his nurse took him and fled. And it happened, as she made haste to flee, that he fell and became lame. His name was Mephibosheth (2 Sam. 4:4)

His name means "destroying shame" and there is no way of knowing in the biblical record about him as to what that means. However, as we look further into his life, shame may have characterized his upbringing as in those days a cripple was in effect treated as a non-person and thereby, he apparently lived a life of personal shame. The meaning of his name is relevant to this study as shame is one of the effects of a life of addiction and alcoholism.

Guilt tells me I have done something wrong… Shame tells me I am something wrong.[8] (Sheila Walsh)

Mephibosheth may have felt he did something wrong in becoming a cripple and certainly would have felt shame as a result.

3. He was abandoned.

Many roots of addiction go back to a loss: a loss of self-esteem, of life security, of family, of purpose resulting in both actual and feelings of abandonment. "Mo" lost the more important things in life: his father Jonathan, his grandfather, and probably his mother and grandmother. The location where King David found him denoted a place of loneliness, a far distance from living in a King's Palace for the first five years of his life. Many roots of addiction go back to losses.

4. It is unknown what he understood of God.

With little information to go on we can only assume that between the age of five until the time King David showed kindness to him, he as an Israelite may or may not have much religious training. Having lost his father Jonathan and grandfather Saul at such an early age and being crippled was a stigma that very well may have left him wondering why his life was not a pleasant one. He may very well had to hide the fact of his connection to royalty.

I found that many who grew up in a dysfunctional family saw God as dysfunctional in His relationship to them. If this is the case, it may make your decision to turn your will over to God as you understood Him difficult. If that's the case, draw inspiration from others who have known Him and hopefully you will see the good and their knowledge of God to be helpful to you.

At this point in the 12 Steps it is important that you come to understand God more fully so you will turn your life over to Him.

> As we surrender our lives and stop carrying the burdens of our past, we will begin to feel better about ourselves. The more we learn to trust in the Lord, the more we will trust ourselves and expand that trust to others. Our decision to choose God's way will restore us to the fullness

of life.[9] *(The Twelve Steps For Christians.* Note: this book is a good supplement for those leading a 12 Step small group)

5. **Mephibosheth was given the gift of kindness, and in so doing, was given a powerful example of God's grace and care for him despite how hard his life had been.**

When David became King, one of the first things he did was to fulfill a promise to his special friend, Jonathan (Mo's father). David said, "Is there anyone of the house of Saul to whom I can show kindness for Jonathan's sake." (2 Samuel 9:1) He was told about Mephibosheth living in Lo-Debar and David had him brought to him in the same palace where he grew up.

We get a picture of Mephibosheth's mentality and his self-esteem as he came before David, bowing down before him probably with knees shaking. After all, his grandfather had tried to kill David and Mo was tied to Saul's kingdom. We might label David's act of kindness as being "surprised by grace." I'm sure it was an overwhelming surprise to

Mephibosheth. In this case, King David is a type of Christ who seeks and saves those who are lost.

6. We should all come to understand David's kindness—he showed the depths of God's grace and mercy to one who felt undeserving.

Note Mephibosheth's response to David's proposed kindness. David said to him, "Don't be afraid." (2 Samuel 9:70) He then promised to restore to him the belongings of his grandfather, Saul. David also said, "You will always eat with me at my table."

As amazing as this is in regards to God's grace offered to Mephibosheth, he could not trust even the King. Maybe because of the hurts you have experienced and also inflicted on others you may find it hard to accept other's love towards you; even God's. Mo responded to this kindness, saying to David, "Why should you care about me? I'm worth no more than a dead dog?" (2 Samuel 9:8 CEV)

I call this the *dead dog* mentality of the wounded. The end story here is this: when Mephibosheth ate at the King's table no one could see he was crippled. Grace covers our sin, our lameness, our hurts, and our wounds. (See also the commentary on 2 Samuel, Chapter 9 in my *Challenge Study Bible*.)

FOLLOW UP REFLECTIONS ON STEP 3

1. Have you made the decision to turn your life over to God? If so, why?

2. Describe your past and present understanding of what you feel God can do for you? Explain.

3. Would you find it difficult to turn control of your life over to God? Be honest in answering this question.

4. How would you describe, "Carrying the burden of your past"?

5. What do you think Mephibosheth meant by referring to himself as, "A dead dog"?

FEEDBACK FROM A PARTICIPANT OF STEP 3

This statement "as we understood Him" sounds like we can decide who God is and how we want to deal with Him. I disagree if that's what it means. As I stated in the previous step, I made a willful decision to surrender to God because I did not have any other options for healing. That decision meant trusting Him with everything. Before I came to Teen Challenge, I was living in a room in Corona, Queens. I was at the lowest point in my life. My ex-wife was divorcing me. I wasn't able to see my children and I felt like I was hopeless and useless in life. Everything I had ever heard about me being "good for nothing" had become a reality. I even questioned whether it was worth living or not. It was during this season of my life that I looked deep inside and asked myself whether I wanted to continue to live like this. I looked at all the reasons that where worth living for. But most importantly, I looked inside me and came to the conclusion that If I allowed God in, there might be hope for me. —Ray Rosa

A PRAYER TO PRAY

"Lord God, I am by faith getting to know You even as I pray to know You more and more. To the best of my ability I offer myself to You to make me what You want me to be by Your will. Help me to give myself more fully to You as You reveal Yourself to me. Forgive me for self-pity and selfishness and create a new me through Your power. I renounce the old me so I can fully embrace Your will."

A PROMISE TO CLAIM

Beloved friends, what should be our proper response to God's marvelous mercies? To surrender yourselves to God to be his sacred, living sacrifices. And live in holiness, experiencing all that delights his heart. For this becomes your genuine expression of worship.

(Romans 12:1 The Passion Translation)

4

SEARCHING... INVENTORY

STEP 4: Made a *searching* and fearless moral *inventory* of ourselves.

Let us test and examine our ways. Let us turn back to the Lord. (Lamentations 3:40 NLT)

> Sometimes we don't recognize ourselves until we judge another and hear the Holy Spirit resound within our hearts, "You are that person."[10] (Beth Moore)

The best biblical example of this Step 4 is found in the Parable of the Prodigal Son. He was like many who experience "the pleasures of sin for a season." His season did not turn out well. He was wise enough to take a moral inventory of where his choice to do life on his own terms led him. Many do not. They prolong seeking a change. Usually they deal with their problems by changing addresses, which is called "the geographic cure." Others change treatment programs. Some change relationships, thinking another person will help them cope with life better.

I have described a way of life living in a cycle of treatment programs this way. It's like a car wash. Your car or truck gets dirty. So you go through the water washing tunnel and come out the other end maybe in 3-5 minutes and the vehicle is clean. But you know your vehicle is going to get dirty again, and back to the car wash again. It's a fact of life. So addiction works somewhat the same way. It's not 3 minutes, but 30 days or more. But you know you're going to use again and be back to the therapeutic tunnels again. It's a fact of life for the addict.

The Prodigal changed his mind. He saw what his bad choices had done for him. We make our choices and they turn around and make us, for better or worse. The Prodigal did both. Change began when he took moral inventory:

1. "He began to be in want."

His *before* life when compared to his *present* life was the difference between being full and being empty. Or, to but it another way, it was the difference between being a fool and being wise. The road back from being in *want* is to want something better—to want to be restored to sanity from insanity.

You have heard of hitting rock bottom. It's the place you will begin the process upward as you turn to God, the Rock at your bottom. There is a wonderful promise in the famous Psalm 23: "The Lord is my shepherd; I shall not want." You will not "want" the old life of emptiness, of pigpen living, of not enjoying a full course meal. The following describes the life of addiction for the addicts: "He [the Prodigal] would gladly have filled his stomach with the pods that the swine ate." (Luke 15:16)

2. He tried the geographic cure: "He went and joined himself to a citizen of that country."

Misery loves company. "Don't be fooled by those who say such things, [eat and drink for tomorrow we die!] for 'bad company corrupts good character.'" (1 Corinthians 15:32-33 NLT) Eventually, Prodigals find themselves around others who are a reflection of themselves. Often what they see is an even worse version of themselves before they make "a searching and fearless inventory of ourselves." It is good to see others who are in a worse mess for that is the direction the Prodigal was heading. Apparently, he did not like to see where he was headed.

3. "No one gave him anything."

Prodigals and addicts are very self-centered. It is every man and woman for themselves when in a place fit for pigs. Perhaps that is where the phrase "pigging out" came from. Selfishness is sin personified. A life lived only for self will cut you off from people of compassion who desire to help the fallen. But you have to head in their direction by swallowing pride and heading towards the Light.

4. "He came to himself."

One of the most difficult decisions for anyone, no matter their lifestyle, is to see themselves as they really are when it's not a pretty picture. We often take a moral inventory of others much easier than ourselves. If we are to change, we need to know and admit what needs to be changed in us. Until such a person takes a step back and sees the person they have become—and does not like that person—they will remain who they are.

"Moral inventory" is a most difficult exercise especially if we have lived in denial for a long time. We can come to accept the worse version of ourselves. The good thing is that God loves us in spite of our flaws, moral failures, and the dirt in our lives. He comes to clean house because that's the only kind of house He's willing to live in.

5. The Prodigal makes a life-changing decision: "I will arise and go to my father."

He knew what his father was like: loving, caring, and forgiving. You may not yet know Father God as He is. Surround yourself with others who know that God is like the father of the Prodigal. Listen to them talk about their Father-God. He wants to be your Father. If you were raised with no understanding of God as Father, either because He was never a part of your upbringing, or God was portrayed as someone to fear in an unhealthy way, it may take time to learn that He is much different and much better than what you thought. The Prodigal called his father "my father." God will have that same relationship with you if you let Him.

6. The door back into the Father's graces is when we say, "Father, I have sinned against heaven and You."

What the son did is called *repentance.* The Prodigal admitted he had sinned "against heaven" and "before you," meaning his father. Repentance needs to be deep: a sorrow for how our decisions affect father, mother, siblings, family and so on. But, the root problem is disobedience towards heaven and God.

> Jeremiah 17:9-10 says, "The human heart is the most deceitful of all things, and desperately wicked. Who really knows how bad it is? But I, the Lord, search all hearts and examine motives. I give all people their due rewards, according to what their actions deserve." (NLT)

Note that God here does a moral inventory of us all and these two verses tell us the results. When we then, in return, take an inventory of ourselves according to what God requires of us, this is the way to restoration.

7. **The Prodigal's final step back to his father was his humility:** "I am no longer worthy to be called your son. Make me like one of your hired servants." (Luke 15:19)

The Prodigal did not come back to his father with an entitlement mentality as if his father would be so glad to see him back, and that he felt he was doing his father a favor in returning. Martin Luther said, "He that can humble himself earnestly has already won." Repentance requires humility—they are the twin entry points to receive pardon and peace with God. "The preoccupation with self is the enemy of humility."[11] (Franklin Graham)

> A humble person is not one that thinks little of himself, hangs his head and says, "I'm nothing." Rather, he is one who depends wholly on the Lord for everything, in every circumstance.[12] (David Wilkerson)

FOLLOW UP REFLECTIONS ON STEP 4

1. Have you taken a "fearless moral inventory" of yourself? Describe the results. Be specific!

2. How have you been like the Prodigal when "He began to be in want"?

3. List one or several ways you sought help, but it didn't work. In answering, explain why you think it didn't work.

4. When applying what the Prodigal said about "coming to himself" to yourself, how would you define that?

5. What are the twin entry points in returning to Father God? Explain?

FEEDBACK FROM A PARTICIPANT OF STEP 4

Before I came to Teen Challenge everything I had ever heard about me being "good for nothing" had become a reality. I even questioned whether it was worth living or not. It was during this season of my life that I looked deep inside and asked myself whether I wanted to continue to live like this. I looked at all the things that were worth living for. But most importantly, I looked inside me and concluded that if I allowed God in, there might be hope for me. I had no one to blame but myself for the condition I was in. I alone chose to do drugs. I alone made the decisions that led me to almost being homeless. I was 100% to blame. I have seen others throughout my years of ministry that find it difficult to accept responsibility for doing drugs. No one put a gun to my head and said, "Here, smoke this." I was in second grade when I first smoked cigarettes. I stole them from my grandfather. I was in fourth grade when I first smoked pot, backstage at the Catholic school I attended. I was 15 when I first tried drinking cough syrup and pills. I thought it was cool and made me feel like a leader. I was 18 when I first tried cocaine. All those choices were mine—no one else. They were a part of my moral inventory I had to own up to. I did! —Ray Rosa

A PRAYER TO PRAY

"Dear God, it is I who has made my life a mess, I have done it, but I cannot undo it. My mistakes are mine and I will begin a searching and fearless moral inventory. I will write down my wrongs, but I will also include that which is good. I pray for the strength to complete the task." (From Alcoholics Anonymous, *Twelve Step Prayer*)[13]

A PROMISE TO CLAIM

My heart is hopelessly dark and deceitful,
a puzzle that no one can figure out.
But I, God, search the heart and examine the mind.
I get to the heart of the human.
I get to the root of things.
I treat them as they really are, not as they pretend to be.

(Jeremiah 17:9-10 MSG)

5

ADMITTED... WRONGS

Step 5: Admitted to God,
          To ourselves,
                    And to another human being
                            the exact nature
                                    of our wrongs.

For I acknowledge my transgressions, and my sin is ever before me. (King David, Psalm 51:3)

> Let your confession be as wide as your transgression.[14] (D. L. Moody)

The above Step 5 quote of A.A. text is done purposely to show that this Step is a progressive step downward, hopefully leading to a confession of wrongs committed. The path of wrongs is always downward, something that is often reflected in human nature. In God's kingdom, you have to go down before you can go up.

This step is to swallow pride and take truth serum. It is like cleaning out a closet of debris, dirty laundry, empty whiskey bottles, pill capsules and drug paraphernalia. Perhaps you need to take a picture of it, actually or mentally and share it with a 12 Step mentor or a minister. It is to reveal the truth of what has been the trash of stuff you have built your life on.

> Our lives are like closed houses. All our shameful secrets, embarrassing behaviors, and spoiled hopes lie hidden from view. The air of our lives is stale because we have been afraid to open the doors and windows to anyone else lest we be found out, rejected, or shamed. Step Five is our emergence. When we admit the nature of our wrongs to God, ourselves, and another human being, we are opening the doors and windows of our lives.[15] (From *The Twelves Steps for Christians*)

Ironically, the Bible character we turn to in order to share what this Step is all about is King David. He committed a blatant rooftop look of lust with a neighbor named Bathsheba. As was mentioned in the Introduction, we do not know if David had a lust problem or whether his adultery was a one-time thing. Probably the latter. Nevertheless, he had to deal with it in the manner as anyone who had broken God's commandments and needed to come clean.

Worse for David was the way he initially covered up his sin. He took a lot of downward steps to make it look like Bathsheba's husband had sexual intercourse with his wife when David brough him back from military service to be with her. He was purer than David, and Uriah refused to sleep with his wife while his men were out on the battlefield.

There was no 12 Step or Celebrate Recovery in those days. But there was a Nathan, a prophet who wisely faced David with his sin by piercing his heart with a divine arrow of truth, saying to the King, "Thou art the man!" (2 Samuel 12:7) who did a terrible sin. David did what anyone should do when walking to and through this Step—he admitted his sin saying, "I have sinned against the Lord." What is important is that David admitted he did not just sin before Bathsheba, against her husband, and others. Most importantly, he confessed that he sinned "before the Lord." (2 Samuel 12:13)

As soon as David admitted, submitted, and surrendered to whatever the consequences would be, Nathan gave God's verdict on the matter: "The Lord has put away your sin." The wonderful thing about God's forgiveness is that it came at the exact same time, in the same verse of Scripture when David said he had sinned against the Lord. Psalm 51 was written by David "after he had gone to Bathsheba." In it are a few noteworthy verses that are important for Step 5:

- "Behold, You desire truth in the inward parts, and in the hidden part You will make me to know wisdom." (51:6)

- "Hide Your face from my sins, and blot out my iniquities." (51:9)

- "Do not cast me away from Your presence, and do not take Your Holy Spirit from me." (51:11)

Some contend that Bathsheba was the temptress in this sordid affair, but she was not. A woman in the ancient culture would never refuse a request for the King to see her. The sex no doubt was consensual, but given the culture norms, Bathsheba may have felt she had no choice in the matter.

Though we're forgiven of wrong doing, it does not mean we may not have to pay the consequences of it. For example, those who put poisons in their body can pay for it the rest of their life, suffering from sickness or disease (and I don't mean the disease of alcoholism). In David's case, God's judgement for his sin was the loss of the son that was born from the illicit affair. The other was the damage to his reputation.

A man or woman may sin, but if they admit to it when confronted and they repent, they will not remain in their sin. Confession of wrongs (sin) is not a sign of weakness, but strength, especially if the confessor learns from the sin. David was confronted about his sin and it would have been better that once he had committed it, he confessed it. By not doing so, the cover up led to him being the equivalent to an accessory to murder in the death of Bathsheba's warrior husband.

One of the good things about a 12 Step program or ministry is that it creates a safe place for confession. Churches in general are not good at confrontation. This is why small groups are helpful. If you don't have access to such a place, find a person you trust to share and confess to. In doing so, it is neither good to sugar coat a confession nor go too deep in detail, especially if that would expose another to the incident being shared and confessed in a manner that might hurt someone. Confession wrapped in an excuse is a non-confession. Confession follows conviction; or it should.

David was told, "You are the man" when Nathan shared the story of a rich man refusing to feed a visitor from his own flock, but demanded a poor man to give up his lamb and prepare it as a meal for a hungry traveler. David's "anger was greatly aroused" and he said to Nathan "the man who did this will surely die." (2 Samuel 12:5) Then Nathan trapped David into realizing this was a fictitious story about himself. The prophet said, "Why have you despised the Lord, to do evil in His sight?" (v. 7-9) David was quick to confess and the Lord was just as quick to "put away your sin." (2 Samuel 12:13 NIV) We find David's further response to this in Psalm 51 when he writes:

> "Wash me and I shall be whiter than snow… Restore to me the joy of Your salvation, and uphold me with Your generous Spirit." (51:7, 12)

God's redemptive work on behalf of David was in the birth of Solomon. Some other lessons to be learned from David's sin:

1. One sin leads to another.

David's cover up was as bad as the adultery. Provers 28:13 says, "Whoever conceals their sins does not prosper, but the one that confesses and renounces them finds mercy." It is a biblical truth that whatever is not confessed, cannot be forgiven.

2. Sin is not always a private matter.

Our lives affect many other people, whether or not we are conscious of it. Nathan told the King that in committing this great sin, David had despised the Lord by presuming God would not judge him. Most addicts are so focused on themselves and on getting high they are oblivious to how their moral defects affect others. As the saying goes, "No man is an island." Sin is rarely a private matter—there is collateral damage.

3. The child born to Bathsheba and David died, but God in His mercy gave them a second chance in the birth of Solomon.

There is a mystery in that Solomon was given two names. God told Nathan the name of the second chance child should be "Jedidiah." Yet, they named him "Solomon"? Solomon is the form of the word *shalom*, which means "peace." Jedidiah means "loved by God." David means "beloved one." In the naming of Solomon, it was God's promise that his dynasty would continue through Solomon all of which was a sign of the mercy of God.

4. There is success after sin.

The account in Scripture right after the above-mentioned naming of Solomon, is that David's army went to "Rabbah and captured it. David took the crown from the king's head [of the Ammonite king], and it was placed on his own head." (2 Samuel 12:29-31) That gold crown set with precious stones was worth a very large sum of money. Yes, there is victory and success after confronting sin, confessing it, and walking in godly sorrow over sin.

FOLLOW UP REFLECTIONS ON STEP 5

1. Have you confessed in some manner the exact nature of your wrongs? Note, it is not always best to do it in a group setting. A trusted leader may be best. Or you may feel led to write down the "exact nature of [your] wrongs."

2. You might ask, "If I asked God's forgiveness, why do I need to share my transgressions with another person?" There is reason to choose such a person. (Pray about who to share with. Preferably someone familiar with the 12 Steps. The purpose is to be willing to be accountable to some godly authority.)

3. Read carefully Psalm 51, David's confession. Maybe take notes on it as it applies to you.

4. What do you think David meant when he said, "Against You, You only have I sinned and done what is evil in your sight" when it was obvious that he did it openly before others.

5. What do you want God to do for you in anticipation of looking forward after you have made things right with Him and others? You can explain in brief or at some length. (You may even want to write it down, especially if you're keeping a journal.)

FEEDBACK FROM A PARTICIPANT OF STEP 5

Sometimes it hurts pouring my heart out to staff who would then hang up my dirty laundry for others to see. But in the end, I was healed because I trusted. I was healed because I was open. I was healed because of God's grace. James 5:16 says, "Therefore confess your sins to each other and pray for each other so that you may be healed. The prayer of a righteous person is powerful and effective." It was my confession that opened the doors for God to heal. It was the prayers of those who loved me that moved God's hand in my life. To God be the glory! —Ray Rosa

A PRAYER TO PRAY

"Jesus, I am at one of the most difficult challenges I have ever faced, making an inventory of my admitted character defects. They are open to You—and more. I can't come clean without Your help. Give me strength and courage to share it with others however I may choose to do so. This is a big step I know I need to take, but I can't do it without Your power to do so. I want to do this because I know it's an important part of my recovery. Thank You for hearing and answering my prayer."

PROMISES TO CLAIM

*Before I confessed my sins, I kept it all inside;
my dishonesty devastated my inner life,
causing my life to be filled with frustration,
inexpressible anguish, and misery.
The pain never let up, for your hand of
conviction was heavy on my heart.
My strength was sapped, my inner life dried up like a
spiritual drought within my soul.
Then I finally admitted to you all my sins,
refusing to hide them any longer. I said,
"My life-giving God, I will openly acknowledge my evil
actions." And you forgave me! All at once the guilt
of my sin washed away and all my pain disappeared.*

(Psalm 32:3-5 The Passion Translation)

6

DEFECTS... OF CHARACTER

Step 6: Were entirely ready to have God remove all these defects of character.

Stop imitating the ideals and opinions of the culture around you, but be inwardly transformed by the Holy Spirit through a total reformation of how you think. This will empower you to discern God's will as you live a beautiful life, satisfying and perfect in his eyes. (Romans 12:2 The Passion Translation)

> Being confronted on character issues isn't pleasant. It hurts our self-image. It humbles us. But it doesn't harm us. Loving confrontation protects us from blindness and self-destruction.[16] (Henry Cloud)

The mirror on my visor in my car shows up too many spots on my face. The mirror of God's Word can reveal things in us—defects that need removing. (See James 1:23-24 NIV) We all have wrinkles, defects physically, spiritually, and in our character. Depending on how we live our lives, some defects are deeper and more identifiable to others and less so to ourselves. These character defects can be called shortcomings and that is even the way God defines them. Romans 3:23 says, "For all have sinned and come short of the glory of God." Sin is coming up short of what God intends for how we should live.

We are sinners and sinners sin in various ways. Some worse than others, at least in the eyes of other men and women. But God does not totem pole sin. In His eyes, there are no big sins or little sins. Whatever they are, sin causes us to come up short to living by God's standards. However, we all have types of behavior, attitudes, and actions that cause us not only to come up short with God, but with others. For example, addiction to adult beverages, opioids, and other drugs leads to broken relationships with significant others and perhaps with the law. If we are going to live a changed life, it must begin with a change of behavior, of character.

What are some of the typical behaviors (character defects) of addicts? (1) Manipulation, (2) Lying, (3) Irresponsibility (4) Stealing; either literally or emotionally stealing time with loved ones, employers, and others, (5) Broken promises, (6) Anger, (7) Pride.

Step 6 is not like any other of the first 5 Steps. However, it is connected with Step 3 that says the decision to "turn over our will to God" is required in this process to recovery. Step Six cannot be alone. It requires turning over yourself and your defects (sins) to God, asking Him to remove them. Our part is the humility—the turning over to Him those things we know that are major hinderances to sobriety and living clean and pure before God and others. Step six cannot be done without having first done Step 3—*"turning over our will* to God.

Before God can help us, we must be willing to relinquish self-destructive behavior, and that is possible through God's power and grace. Having defects removed is not done overnight. It is a process. It takes prayer and the study of God's Word to know in what way we need to measure up to His standards. It requires being accountable either to a person, persons, spouse, family, pastor, or a mentor. Loners need not apply for defect removal. It takes group participation. This is why belonging to a community of faith such as a local church or fellowship is so important.

However, do not make the mistake by thinking if you attend a 12 Step or similar group gathering that is all you need. Self-examination is needed on an ongoing basis. Have daily readings in the Bible and Bible help books or Christian books on recovery. Remember some of our defects of character have been deeply engrained in us over years of behavior. Changing is not an overnight process. Be patient with yourself on this journey to wholeness.

The key to completing this Step is surrender. It means stop doing your own thing, your own will. Relinquish yourself, your will to God's control. Resign from being the master, the lord over your life. This is the ultimate recognition of your powerlessness if this Step is to be successful.

Let us now look at the Bible character that helps us do a study of the need to remover a character defect. Jacob is a good example. He was a first-class deceiver, having plotted with his mother to steal his twin brother Esau's birthright. He was a man with two natures. His early years were a mixture of good and bad; more bad than good. He was a manipulator, a deceitful con man. Yet, he found himself with someone he worked for and sought marriage to his daughter—Laban, who out Jacob-ed Jacob, beating him at his own con game.

Jacob also had some inherent good in him. Despite his flaws, he was a man who had a hunger to know and serve

God. We see this at the brook Jabbok. Jacob wrestled with a Man (angel) or better said, the angel wrestled with him. As a result, Jacob said, "I will not let You go until You bless me." (Genesis 32:26) Then Jacob was asked, "What is your name?" (v. 27)

There are two important things about this question. One, I'm sure this heavenly messenger knew Jacob's name. Second, in many biblical accounts, we do not know the time frame. Was there an amount of time between Jacob being asked his name and when he answered, "Jacob." I'd like to think so.

Here is why? What the Man-angel was asking may have been for Jacob to admit his character defect. His name meant "supplanter." A supplanter is defined as "someone or something taking the place of another, as through force, scheming, strategy, or the like." Such was Jacob in scheming to steal his twin Esau of his birthright. In today's language, we would say Jacob was a manipulator, a deceiver, a rogue.

Looking at the question posed to Jacob, "What is your name?" there was, I believe, much more than just asking his name in a manner you and I might be asked our name when meeting someone for the first time. What the Lord was after is a confession of Jacob as to the defects of his character.

When Jacob said his name was "Jacob" he was in essence saying my name is *Jacob* and I have lived up to and down to my name in all its meaning. This was an important step of humility and repentance. Based on this, the Man-Angel said, "Your name shall no longer be called Jacob, but Israel, for you have struggled with God and with men, and have prevailed." (Genesis 32:28) If you have struggled to confess sins, wrongs, and character defects you are in good company. Jacob struggled and prevailed! This is what the 12 Steps is about. It is a heart search. A soul search. A character defect search and an admission to God and others the "exact nature of your wrongs."

After this angel encounter and a reconciliation between Jacob and Esau in which all was forgiven between them, Jacob returned to the Promise Land where he set up an altar as a sign of his spiritual restoration.

FOLLOW UP QUESTIONS AND REFLECTIONS ON STEP 6

1. Do you find it hard just thinking about confessing wrongs to another person? (Pray for strength to do so.)

2. Write down a few things you would confess to someone without showing it to another person. Then tear the paper up, using it as a first step to doing it with someone you feel would be understanding and compassionate.

3. You may need to take time to work up the courage to make an open confession.

4. Confession is not just for Catholics, for the Bible says, "Confess your sins to each other and pray for each other that you may be healed." (James 5:16a)

5. The next Step is a huge one for change and recovery, but in this Step it's about being willing. If you lived all your life up to now being unwilling to accept personal responsibility for your actions, then it's time to let go of your will and let God take over.

FEEDBACK FROM A PARTICIPANT OF STEP 6

At first, I was only willing to give up certain things in my life. I was not "entirely" ready. While I was ready for change, I still had reservations about how much I was willing to surrender. It became evident very quickly that I needed to be all in or this restoration thing would not work. I would say that my character was tainted by my experiences of not being understood. This led to anger, resentment, and lack of empathy for others. I learned protective mechanisms that allowed me to suppress these feelings. The decisions I made on that path was what formed and developed bad character within me. In life, as I have started trusting God, I no longer had to rely on my defenses or self-protective strategies.

I began trusting in God and in effect my character started changing to that of Christ in me. True character change can only happen when we are surrendered to Christ completely. Proverbs 3:5-6 says, "Trust in the Lord with all your heart, and lean not on your own understanding; in all your ways acknowledge Him, and He shall direct your path."
—Ray Rosa

A PRAYER TO PRAY

"Dear God, I am saying yes, I am willing for an inner cleaning. I give up! I can't fight against You and the recovery process and longer. I don't want my defects to defeat me any longer. I want to be honest with myself, and before You, and those who I am willing to be accountable to. Guide me to Your peace and Your healing of my emotions so I can grow up spiritually. I thank You in expectation for the answer to my pray."

Here is an additional prayer to pray from Saint Augustine: "The house of my soul is too small for You to come to it. May it be enlarged by You. It is in ruins; restore it."[17]

A BIBLE PROMISE TO CLAIM

I'm single minded in pursuit of you; don't let me miss the road signs you've posted. I've backed your promises in the vault of my heart so I won't sin myself bankrupt. Be blessed, God; teach me in your ways of wise living.

(Psalm 118:10-12 MSG)

7

REMOVE... SHORTCOMINGS

Step 7: Humbly asked Him to remove our shortcomings.

For all have sinned and fall short of the glory of God. (Romans 3:23)

> We can learn the purpose of God as we fill ourselves with His Word and then look to Him for direction with a surrendered heart.[18] (Jim Cymbala)

This is similar in some ways to Step 6 which dwelt with a person's personal shortfall with God, called sin. This has to do with falling short, or not measuring up to following God's will and His way. The former we might call the sins of transgressions. But in addition, there are sins of omission. One is not doing right and the other is leaving undone the things God requires of us. The latter can lead to sin if God's will is not done.

Step 7 is about spiritual growth. Like Step 6, it also requires surrendering those things that keep us from doing God's will. This may be shame, self-pity, anger, unforgiveness, partial obedience to God and man; and even spiritual laziness. As you go deeper into the things of God, He will begin to reveal more things that need changing. It's like cleaning out a room cluttered with junk. The more you clean, the more you see what needs cleaning. This can be both discouraging and encouraging. No one likes to dig deeper into the part of their life that needs changing. It takes time to see the full extent of our sins and shortcomings. On the other hand, the more you get rid of, the more room there is for God to occupy those places in your life. Forgiveness brings spiritual and emotional health; anger can be replaced with peace; hatred with love; cover up with Light and Truth; and pride with humility.

It is like a person who lives on junk food, bad meals, stale stuff and then they begin sitting at a table with a menu of better food. Get the junk out of your life so God can feed you on His manna and His soul food. Paul said, "Be not drunk with wine wherein is excess, but be filled with the Spirit." (Ephesians 5:18) Change your drinking habits by exchanging a drink of *spirits* to drinking in the Holy Spirit. Change you meds to meditations. Change your pills for the Gos-pill. (Pun intended)

Don't fall for the faulty thinking that makes excuses for bad behavior by saying, "Well, this is just who and what I am." You can get accustomed to living a defective, shortcoming life as if you think the worse part of you is the best part. The worse person is the one who loves the dark part of their life. Gangsters and street hoods revel in who and what they are. You must hate the things that keep you living on either low-level life or a "high" level life (pun also intended).

Where can we look at the Bible to identify with Step 7? I list Peter in this case. Peter was a reed transformed into a rock. The *before* Peter and the *after* Peter were two different people. Here is what to know about the total Peter.

1. He was impulsive, stepping out of the boat to walk on the water with Jesus. (Matthew 14:28)

2. He got carried away on the Mount of Transfiguration and wanted to build memorials there. (Matthew 17:4)

3. He was courageous in his confession that Jesus was the Christ of God. (Matthew 16:16)

And yet! Good men and women, even those who become great as Peter did, can make colossal mistakes. Peter denied the Lord! (Matthew 26:69-75) As Jesus prophesied that Peter would deny Him, when he did, he was immediately broken and "wept bitterly." (26:75)

When Jesus came out of the grave, Peter got up and "arose and ran to the tomb" and became the first disciple to see the empty tomb. For all of Peter's shortcomings, he was quick to make things right with the Lord. It began at the moment when Peter denied the Lord and a rooster crowed three times. As Peter was in the courtyard at Jesus' trial and he denied he knew Jesus, "The Lord looked at Peter" (Luke 22:61) and Peter immediately felt shame, guilt, and remorse. From that point on, Peter began to turn his shortcomings into a long-term commitment to his call to be a fisher of men and one of the greatest of the Apostles.

God is in the reclaiming business. God is the God of second chances. He turns bitter tears and brokenness into making us strong where we have been weak.

Here's some further lessons from the life of Peter:

1. He was willing to take risks!

On one occasion, he saw Jesus walking on the water and he got out of the boat to go to Jesus, miraculously able for a time to walk on water. If you are going to walk out the 12 Steps, it's going to take a faith-risk, asking the Lord to save you. Getting out of the boat is being willing to leave your comfort zone that you have felt most secure in and of the life you have gotten used to and leave it behind to follow Jesus. If you take your eyes off Jesus, you can drown and sink to the bottom from which you will need to come up out of again.

Maybe Peter got caught up in, "Wow, look at me! I can walk on water just like Jesus." In so doing, he might have thought this was more about him than Jesus. Always remember to never take your eyes off the Source of your sobriety and freedom from life-controlling problems. The easiest thing to do is get prideful and take credit for your progress. Apostle Paul, who had every right we might say in the natural to credit himself for his success, said, "Not I, but Christ liveth in me." (Galatians 2:20) A completer of our program said to me about his relapse, "Pastor, as soon as I walked out the door, I looked up and said, 'Okay God, I'll take it from here.'" Self-determination almost always leads to a relapse.

2. Peter made a bold confession of faith.

Peter apparently learned his lesson, for when Jesus asked His disciples the question as to what others were saying about Him, he said, "You are the Messiah, the Son of the living God." (Matthew 16:16) Then Jesus said to the man who once took his eyes off Jesus and began to sink in the water as if a rock: "I say to you that you are Peter, and on this rock, I will build My church." (Matthew 16:18) Peter's confession is one of the most famous in the Bible. When you make the same confession, it will hold back the powers of hell that come against believers. Think of it—you can go from *rock bottom* to standing on the *Solid Rock,* Jesus.

FOLLOW UP QUESTIONS
AND REFLECTIONS ON STEP 7

1. Since humility is necessary in all the 12 Steps, share what might be a struggle for you in "asking Him to remove your shortcomings."

2. As you have committed to work the 12 Steps, what defects of character do you realize you have yet to confess to God? (You can keep this to yourself, or share if you so desire.)

3. What benefits have you experienced thus far in doing these Steps?

4. What negative thoughts do you need to let go to reach the goal of sobriety and a changed life?

5. What some new and good ways of thinking have you achieved since doing these Steps?

FEEDBACK FROM A PARTICIPANT OF STEP 7

On September 2, 1945, the Japanese signed a surrender on the deck of the USS Missouri in Tokyo Bay. This document is what is called, "The Instrument of Surrender." It was Japan surrendering unconditionally to the allied forces. They would cease all hostilities, release prisoners of war, and ensure that none of its commanders retaliated against the allied forces. It was a complete surrender that saved Japan from total destruction. When I was on drugs, I was at war with God. I was an enemy combatant. I was fighting against God as a soldier for the enemy, Satan. I surrendered to God, but first I needed to acknowledge what I had done wrong. I then signed an unconditional surrender document when I made Him King of my life. I also gave Him the seat of the throne on which I sat for many years. I recognized that I was not good at ruling my life. I needed a righteous, holy King to Lord over me. And that He did. He sat on the throne and from there, destroyed all my enemies (Psalm 18). For in humility, we find true worth, a Christ-like spirit, a heavenly birth. And in the depths of our humble plea, we discover the grace that sets us free. —Ray Rosa

A PRAYER TO PRAY

"Lord, You know all about me. I cannot hide anything from You. Yet I know You love me and want what is best for me. Help me to surrender my all to You. If I stumble, stick with me. I now know I was not made to be lost in my sins. I also know I didn't find You—You found me. So I give myself to You for You to finish the work You began in me. Thank You! Thank You! I know I don't deserve this, so I accept Your favor and grace towards me. I love the fact I am now one of Your chosen ones."

A BIBLE PROMISE TO CLAIM

Go turn to God! Give up your sin,
and you will be forgiven.
Then the time will come when the Lord
will give you fresh strength.
He will send you Jesus, His chosen Messiah.

(Acts 3:19-20 CEV)

8

MAKE... AMENDS

Step 8: Make a list of all persons we had wronged, and became willing to make amends to them all.

In prayer there is a connection between what God does and what you do. You can't get forgiveness from God, for instance, without also forgiving others. If you refuse to do your part, you cut yourself off from God's part. (Matthew 6:14-25 MSG)

Be kind and compassionate to one another, forgiving each other, just as in Christ God forgave you. (Ephesians 4:32 NIV)

It is necessary to understand that we need a vertical relationship with God and a horizontal relationship with others. You can have that upward and strong connection with God, yet a week outward connection with others, especially those with whom you have hurt to one degree or another. Jesus said the two Great Commands are, "to love God with all your heart...a second is equally important: Love your neighbor as yourself." (Matthew 22:37-39 NLT)

> In Step Eight we begin to grow up... [by taking] responsibility for our actions without consideration for the wrongs done to us by others. Throughout these Steps we have been dealing with own stuff.[19] (The Twelves Steps for Christians)

As hard as it can be to humble ourselves before God and ask forgiveness for the depth of our wrongs (such as in a group setting or doing so in private prayer), to do so before specific people or persons we have wronged is one of the greatest challenges of all. But it can also be one of the greatest cleansings and loss of weight—the "weight" of guilt and shame. Note this Step 8 is about being "willing to make amends to them all."

The next Step, Step 9 is going to such persons and asking forgiveness in the hopes of healing the hurts we have caused them. But first, there needs to be a *willingness* to make things right with loved ones and significant others. Making amends is one Step at a time. One person said, "As soon as I was willing to make amends—and it was a long process to get to that point with a lot of group meetings and mentoring—but when my will to do so changed, I was given *will power* by the grace of God to do it.

> Becoming willing to make amends does not mean that we have to like the idea. To be sure, the task ahead will probably be difficult with those who have suffered because of our past behavior... Quite likely, they may not be happy to see us, much less sympathize with our purpose.[20] *(The Gospel and the Twelves Steps)*

Nevertheless, the benefit of making amends can go a long way to mending broken relationships. It may be a surprise to some that I choose an unnamed person as an example of making amends. It is a woman of which we have no details of her making amends. To do so we need to read between the lines to see what she did while going to certain persons (all men) to right some wrongs. She is known famously as the Woman at the Well, Jacob's Well, which is located outside the city of Sychar in Samaritan (John chapter 4). Thus, she is known as the Samaritan woman.

Jesus has what appeared to be a casual encounter with her, but all His encounters are meaningful and often miraculous in their results. We get an indication of this when John, the author of this gospel says, "He needed to go through Samaria." (John 4:4) In those days, any respected Jew would not go *through Samaria,* but travel around it, leaving Jerusalem and heading east, then north to avoid going through a region where there were deep hostilities towards Samaritans and Jews, and vice versa.

Religious and racial prejudices separated Jews and Samaritans. The latter were descendants of foreigners who had entered Israel and began intermixing and marrying with Israelites. They did not accept the teaching of the Old Testament after the Pentateuch. They claimed that God should be worshipped on Mount Gerizim halfway between Jerusalem and Nazareth.

Jesus was sensitive to this issue in that He crossed two cultural divides in talking to a woman, and a Samaritan, no less. So Jesus sent his disciples into a village to buy food while He conversed with the Woman at the Well. (John 4:8) Even the woman was surprised that Jesus would ask her for a drink of water. (v. 9)

What should also be of interest in this encounter is when it took place. At the 6th hour, or noon. Typically, women went to get water for their household needs early in the morning before the heat of the day made such a chore difficult because of the blistering heat. She avoided going to the well at the typical hour because she was an outcast. Jesus engaged in what we might call casual or friendship evangelism, simply asking for a drink of water, much to her surprise. She questioned Jesus asking of her, being such a person as she was as we soon learn. It did not take Jesus long to zero in on her lifestyle.

Here is an evangelism tip: connect before judging another. Jesus offered her, much to her surprise, "living water." Jesus used something natural to lead to the supernatural. At first, she did not understand and asked Him a question from a historical context: "Are you greater than our father Jacob?" Jacob had frequented in the past the exact same well. (v. 11). Jesus then arouses the woman's curiosity saying that He had water by which she would never thirst again. Then Jesus touched a nerve in this woman's lifestyle by asking her to go call her husband. Turns out, she had had five husbands and was living common-law, as we would define it today, with man number six.

Jesus then introduced Himself to her as the Messiah (vs. 25-26). She already knew Jesus was a prophet by the fact that He knew she had five failed marriages and was living as an unmarried woman, with yet another man (that being unheard of, even in her religion and culture). He then went from being a prophet to being, in her understanding, the Messiah of the Jews—and it changed her life.

She then rushes off to her village. Something struck me about how the King James Version in this story describes the event at this point. It says, "The woman then left her waterpot, went her way into the city, *and said to the men...*" (John 4:28) This is what leaped off the pages of the Bible to me: *"and said to the men."* What men? I believe she may have gone to all six men and told them about Jesus, and in so doing shared with them saying, "Come, see a Man who told me all things I ever did. Could this be the Christ?" (v. 29) This was a powerful admission on her part. Sort of like Jacob saying, "Yes, I am a Jacob." In her case, she was saying she was admitting the kind of woman she was, treating husbands as disposable persons.

Within the context of this scriptural account, it seems that this woman could very well have been trying to make amends for her behavior. She must have been very convincing about her encounter with Jesus when she declared, "He told me all things I ever did" and in her question, saying, "Could this be the Christ?" (v. 29) John 4:39 says, "Many of the Samaritans from the town believed in Him because of the woman's testimony."

According to the dictionary, amends means "something done or given by a person to make up for a loss or injury he or she has caused." In the case of this woman, there's no doubt there were two sides of her marriage break ups, but because of her encounter with Jesus, she must have admitted her part of the break ups and this can be defined as making amends.

One of the most power things about admitting character defects is it often leads to making amends through asking for forgiveness. Forgiveness is a two-way street. We go down the street and go to the cross of Christ and ask for His forgiveness of our sins. Then we return and go back up the street and go to those we have hurt. What a wonderful freedom from guilt, shame, and loneliness can be experienced from this. In simple terms, forgiveness is in effect cancelling a debt.

What about the wrongs against us? If it is the same person, very often that person both receives our forgiveness and forgives in return. But if they do not, that is up to them and we can only do what is required of us in the matter of asking for forgiveness. Unreturned forgiveness needs to be left in the hands of the Lord. It has been said that some of the sweetest words in whatever the language is, is "I forgive you."

Some scholars contend that a revival broke out in the town from this one remarkably changed life. This is further advanced as a theory because "They [the townspeople] urged Him to stay with them, *and He stayed there two days."* (John 4:40) The next verse says, "Many more believed because of His own word." (4:41) It must have tested the patience of the disciples that Jesus would spend that amount of time in Samaria where it had already been recorded that "the Jews had no dealings with Samaritans." (John 4:9) What an amazing two days! Making amends can open a door into other's hearts, even to a family, even an entire community.

FOLLOW UP QUESTIONS AND REFLECTIONS ON STEP 8

1. How have you experienced shame as apparently this woman had?

2. Can you name one or more defects of character you need to ask God to help you remove?

3. Are you ready to have Him remove at least one character flaw? If so, name it. If not, why not?

4. Can you write out or say a prayer to God of how you want Him to help you in this Step?

5. Can you picture your sharing with others—family, friends, co-workers as this woman did? If not, why?

FEEDBACK FROM A PARTICIPANT OF STEP 8

I gained the ability to comprehend the pain and harm I had inflicted upon my loved ones. I had been entirely self-centered, incapable of understanding or caring about the feelings of others, particularly the harm I caused to those closest to me. However, as I began to regain my senses, I made it a priority to reconcile with the individuals I had harmed, including my parents, ex-wife, children, relatives, and friends. I even felt compelled to settle any outstanding debts I owed to creditors. The healing process unfolded as I started to empathize with the pain I had caused, which led to feelings of remorse and a profound sense of brokenness within my spirit and conscience. This brokenness prompted me to seek forgiveness for my wrongdoing. —Ray Rosa

A PRAYER TO PRAY

"Lord, the truth is I'm finding it difficult to face those I have hurt—but I know I need to do this, not just because I'm committed to this process, but also because I know I need to do this for my own good and the good of those I have hurt. So, please help me. My will is weak. My fears are strong. Help me so my feelings don't keep me from doing the right thing. You said if anyone lack wisdom to ask You. So here I am now asking. I need the words to say and the power to say them. Amen!"

A PROMISE FROM THE BIBLE TO CLAIM

And whenever you stand praying,
if you find that you carry something in your heart
against another person, release him and forgive him
so that your Father in heaven will also release you
and forgive you of your faults.

(Mark 11:25 The Passion Translation)

9

AMENDS....TO [SPECIFIC] PEOPLE

STEP 9: Make direct amends to such people whenever possible, except when to do so would injure them or others.

Therefore, if you are offering your gift at the altar and there remember that your brother or sister has something against you, leave your gift there in front of the altar. First go and be reconciled to them; then come and offer your gift. (Matthew 5:23-24 NIV)

> "The strongest person always initiates the reconciliation and thus, the peace." (Source unknown)

Both Steps 8 and 9 are about amends: eight is being "willing" to do so. Step 9 is making personal direct contact with those that we may have hurt. This should be done with sensitivity and understanding. It requires changing our behavior in order to have the right to make amends. Fear can cause you to procrastinate and not make a necessary approach.

> When we extend love to others, we diminish their power over us and expend God's forgiveness, which he has so graciously given us.[21] *(The Twelve Steps For Christians)*

Making personal contact should be done with perceptivity and it may take time for the other person to be willing to meet with you; or even receive you and hear you out. It's good in some cases to use a third party in order to do so. A change in your behavior in general and especially if specifically to that person can pave the way for them to be open to receiving you. In efforts to repair a relationship, it takes loving humility and it may involve having to hear some harsh things said to you. What can at first seem an unsuccessful attempt to seek forgiveness should not cause you to give up. I've seen people ask forgive and were turned away; yet they went back to that person a second time and healing began.

As long as we're estranged from someone, they can seem to have a power over us that is not good for our mental and spiritual health. Seeking forgiveness can break the stronghold between yourself and the person you have wronged. They can end up being unforgiving, unyielding to a reconciliation and that puts them in a position in which the wronged is wrong. If the person is a Christian, allow the Holy Spirit time to deal with them. Remember, forgiveness is a process whether you are on the giving end of it or hoping to receive it.

Making amens often will mean being rejected, but be determined to continue to pursue reconciliation. In the end, if it happens, a huge weight will drop off you. It is like getting freed from the prison you have been in regarding them and once you forgive, they may end up in their own kind of prison of unforgiveness if they reject you. The healing of broken relationships is a powerful experience when choosing to make a wrong right.

I recall helping a woman in England at the gravesite of her father, on my recommendation, that she forgave him postmortem. The back story is that her father was a minister and she discovered later in life on her birth certificate that her mother was not her biological mother. She carried an anger toward her father all through his and her life, including after his death. When I learned how deeply this affected her emotionally and spiritually, I gently suggested she go to his gravesite. I said I would go with her with no conditions on her part or mine. So, we did so. And she made amends posthumously with her father, a very freeing moment and experience for her.

There is a great Bible story of a man that made amends that involved making financial restitution. His name was Zacchaeus. As a Jew, he was considered a traitor to his people because he worked for the Roman government collecting taxes for them, and in the process became very rich. Apparently, Zacchaeus had heard about Jesus and when Jesus entered Jericho where he lived, he was curious to see Him. But he had two problems—the crowd was large and he was of such a short stature that he was blocked from seeing Jesus. He saw the path Jesus was taking and ran ahead and climbed up a sycamore tree, giving a clear view of Jesus when He reached that point. If he thought in doing this, he could be anonymous, he was wrong. How ironic that one can attend an Alcoholic Anonymous or a similar group to feel safe from others, knowing who and what you are, but you can never be anonymous from the Lord. So it was with Zacchaeus.

> Luke 19: 5-6 NIV says, "Jesus reached the spot, and said to him, 'Zacchaeus, come down

immediately. I must stay at your house today.' So he came down at once and welcomed Him gladly."

That probably was an understatement. The little man may have fallen out of the tree in fright. Here's what we can assume and know, both what and why Zacchaeus responded as he did to Jesus' invitation.

1. This was a man full of guilt and shame.

He knew he was wrong on several accounts: A Jew working for the Romans and cheating the taxpayers in the process. It is not much of an assumption that when he heard Jesus was coming through Jericho that something was drawing him to see Him, even if from a distance. There is no distance between a person filled with shame and guilt and Jesus.

Jesus is the bridge between guilt and shame being erased, and when you come to Him you get a fresh start as if what you did never happened. Or, you will remember it as you should; not to be condemned, but as a warning not to repeat the offense. With every new remembrance of a wrong you committed with someone, can come another time of grace and forgiveness. Not every wrong committed to another may need your seeking amends; only those that weigh heavy on your heart and of those who you have access to ask their forgiveness.

    Matthew 5:23-24 is quoted at the beginning of this chapter. Jesus was saying there are occasions when before coming to Him, we should first go to another who we know we have wounded and ask forgiveness. This then opens the door and access for our prayers to be answered, even if the prayer is something other than how we injured another. Jesus was addressing in this teaching those who were his followers. This is a principal of discipleship. Once we have made things right with Jesus, it follows we should make things right with others. Doing right things is not about earning salvation. It is about "working out our salvation with fear and trembling." (Philippians 2:12)

2. Jesus, in inviting Himself to Zacchaeus' home, was taking the initiative in wanting a relationship with a known sinner.

Jesus in saving Zacchaeus referred to him as "a son of Abraham." (Luke 19:9) In doing so, first for Zacchaeus' sake and other Jews who might have heard this said, Jesus was making it clear no one is saved on the basis of ethnic background, or by doing good deeds. We are saved by God's grace and our trust in Him.

In working many years with addicts, I found at times for those who were raised in the church that their Bible knowledge became a source of pride for them. You would think this would make it easier for them to do the 12 Steps, but it can be the opposite. The very fact that Jesus went to Zacchaeus' house sent a powerful message that "the Son of man came to seek and save the lost." (Luke 19:9) That was Jesus' last word in this Bible account, and it's the last word everyone needs to hear when coming to Christ. No matter how we or others perceive us to be a "sinner" this very fact qualifies us for salvation. (See Luke 19:7)

3. Salvation will always have the evidence of a changed life.

At the end of Jesus' visit, Zacchaeus stood up and made a vow to Jesus (and perhaps a few of the disciples) that he was going to give half of his property to the poor and pay back fourfold those he had cheated. (Luke 19:8). This was the true evidence of a changed life. Making amends is making right wrongs and in Zacchaeus's case, putting a dollar amount attached to it as evidence of that change.

AMENDS....TO [SPECIFIC] PEOPLE

FOLLOW UP QUESTIONS AND REFLECTIONS ON STEP 9

1. Can you identify with some of Zacchaeus' fears and insecurities?

2. Have you ever felt like God was calling you to come out of your hidden place to come to Him with your problems?

3. You may not have cheated others out of money as Zacchaeus did, but did you cheat people in other ways? If so, explain.

4. Begin to make a list of those you many need to make amends to, even if you're not ready to actually do it yet. Making a list is a start.

5. Choose one person you feel you need to make amends to and write out briefly what you might say. Then prayerfully ask God to help you to actually go to the person and do so.

FEEDBACK FROM A PARTICIPANT OF STEP 9

I made it a priority to approach those whom I had hurt, acknowledging that, in certain cases like my ex-wife, my apologies were insufficient and arrived too late. Nevertheless, for others, expressing remorse helped pave the way for healing and reconciliation. I believed that their healing was more crucial than mine, and I genuinely desired to contribute to their restoration. I recognized that my actions during my addiction were unequivocally wrong, and I was prepared to accept the consequences. However, I acknowledged that it was unfair to those I had hurt, and that compelled me to assist in their healing process. —Ray Rosa

A PRAYER TO PRAY

"Jesus, I want to be a Zacchaeus, to take a bold step and ask (insert a name or names here) to forgive me for the pain and sorrow I have caused them. I do this in obedience to Your commands and leave the results in Your hands. I know I have been forgiven much, so now I need to go to others and ask their forgiveness. I know I need to do this in obedience to You!"

AMENDS....TO [SPECIFIC] PEOPLE

A PROMISE IN THE BIBLE TO CLAIM

Never pay back evil with more evil.
Do things in such a way that everyone
can see you are honorable.
Do all that you can to live in peace with everyone.

(Romans 12:17-17 NLT)

10

CONTINUE... INVENTORY

STEP 10: Continued to take personal inventory and when we were wrong, promptly admitted it.

If ye continue in my word, then are ye my disciples indeed; and ye shall know the truth, and the truth shall make you free. (John 8:31 KJV)

> God has infinite attention to give each one of us. You are as much alone with Him as if you were the only being He created.[22] (C.S. Lewis)

When a person has a conversion experience and makes real changes in how they live, they reach a point of blessing, success, and danger. The danger is to tell God, "Thank You. But now I can take it from here." They are like the man mentored to be a successful financial investor and he reached a point where he's made some good choices resulting in some good paydays. So he cuts himself off from his mentor and teacher. Then he went out on his own and fails miserably when recommending an investment for one of his clients that lost him a lot of money. It happens all the time. The mentor would have kept this do-it-myself friend from such a wrong decision.

Worse is when a commitment is made to seek help for a life-controlling problem by enrolling in a residential faith-based ministry, a 12 Step small group class, or some other discipleship ministry, and then not crossing the finish line. Jesus is the beginning and the end of our faith journey. (See Hebrews 12:2) To forsake the One who is the reason for a successful recovery is to be unwise at best and a fool at worst. Proverbs says, "The way of a fool is right in his own eyes, but he who heeds counsel is wise." (Proverbs 12:15)

One of the most important but simple words in the Bible is "Continue." Finish what you start. See a thing through. Keep on keeping on. Jesus said, "If ye continue in my word, then are ye my disciples indeed." (John 8:31 KJV) You can get comfortable with the new you and without realizing, begin to do things as the old you. The alcoholic thinks he can drink in moderation only to learn there's no such thing as 'moderation' except when eating a meal. The hardcore cocaine addict thinks he can smoke weed only to find himself back in the garden of weeds in which one smoke leads to another and worse.

Step 10 is about the need for continual spiritual growth. If you are in A.A., Celebrate Recovery, Living Free or some other small group, don't be so quick to leave it, if for no other reason to encourage others towards the path you have been on. Step 10 is critical on the path to full recovery. If you have done the Steps seriously and made full disclosure of your character defects/sins, you will have reached a point when you can either think you can now strike out on your own without God, without mentors, and without becoming a part of the larger family of God. I guarantee you this will be a huge mistake.

Getting clean and sober is not just getting rid of the bad stuff in your life, but replacing it with the good things of God. That is a process—the process of continued spiritual, emotional, and moral growth which is obedience to God's commands and will. By the way, you do not need to understand the way of obedience to be obedient. In time, you will understand.

In the great Bible story of the Israelite's deliverance from their 400 years of bondage, He brought them *out* to bring them *in* to His inheritance; that is, the Promise Land.

It was going to take time for the people of God to come into possession of their inheritance and along the way there would be critical lessons to learn. Those in recovery are meant to come to a place of being *recovered*. Don't buy into the theory that you can only hope that addiction goes into remission. God is a God of transformation. He wants to bring you into wholeness, not a recovery from which you never graduate.

    The continual path requires daily contact with God and working the biblical faith principles of the Steps. Who then can we focus on as a good example of continuing the path of spiritual growth? I return to the disciple Peter and his struggles as a follower of Jesus. You would think his commitment increased after the resurrection of Jesus. He was the first to run to the tomb to see Jesus was not there, but after that he went back to the family fishing business. You would have thought Jesus' resurrection would have sealed Peter's commitment to the Lord. Apparently, it did not!

> John 21:3 says, "Simon Peter, said to them [the other disciples] 'I am going fishing.' They said to him, 'We are going with you.'"

Bible commentators speculate as to why in such a historical, miraculous moment of Jesus' resurrection, why Peter went back to the fishing business and taking some disciples with him? Some commentators believe Peter was backing away from his commitment to Christ; or at best, was waiting for more instructions. So he went to do what best he knew how to do; go commercial fishing. My view is that Peter and all the disciples were looking for Jesus to make Himself King and overthrow the Roman rule. If this be so, it was a case of disappointment in Jesus; like some who follow Jesus today with the attitude of, "What's in it for me?"

Peter did have an encounter with Jesus as he came in from an unsuccessful fishing venture (John 21:4-21) This seemed to bring Peter back on his continued path with Jesus. Peter's restoration, if it might be called that, is revealed in the two epistles he wrote. However, the Peter that became a different and changed man is recorded in the book of Acts.

1. Peter changed from being self-centered to others centered.

Note the *before* Peter. In Matthew 20:20-21, the mother of James and John appealed to Jesus to let their sons be in high positions when they thought Jesus was going to overthrow Roman rule. This upset the other ten disciples as it was every man for himself in the context of what was anticipated as Jesus the King (like David) would set up His Kingdom. Peter, like the rest of the disciples, where me-centered. Ironically, some who go through the 12 Steps as addicts and alcoholics are still very self-centered.

Then we have the *after* Peter. The Day of Pentecost drew a large crowd in Jerusalem, giving the disciples a golden opportunity to preach the gospel. The Scripture says in Acts 2:14, "Then Peter stood up *with the eleven*" to explain what was happening in the coming of the Holy Spirit; and he called for repentance at the closing of his message. About 3,000 did so and became a part of the new Jesus movement. We might say the disciples were 'with-nesses' with Peter giving voice to the message of salvation for all.

What happened to Peter? He was filled with the Holy Spirit and was radically changed. What a testimony it was to have the disciples in unity "standing up [together] with the eleven." No longer every man for himself. Is this the kind of change you are experiencing?

2. Peter's courage!

Acts 4:13 says, "When they [the religious rulers in Jerusalem] saw the courage of Peter and John and realized they were unschooled, ordinary men, they were astonished and they took note that these men had been with Jesus." (NIV)

Remember during Jesus' trial, Peter denied he was one of His disciples. He went from being ashamed to identify himself as a follower of Christ to a man of conviction and courage. Courage is not the absence of fear, but acting in spite of it. When the disciples had been with Jesus, even those who do not follow Him recognize courage when they see it. It has been said that it takes just as much courage to sit and listen to someone as it is to stand up and speak your mind. A German proverbs says, "More things are done through courage than through wisdom."

3. Peter's relapse of courage!

In Acts 14:11-21 in Antioch Peter showed weakness in wanting to be a people-pleaser. When he was with Gentile converts, he ate meat offered to idols which was not an issue with Gentiles. But then, when he was with Jewish believers, Peter was afraid of what they would think so he stopped eating with the Gentiles. Paul confronted him on this. Even a man of God can become a people-pleaser.

I've seen pastors preach to please compromising Christians. I've seen leaders try to please staff or board members on two sides of an issue, thus behaving like a wishy-washy politician instead of a Christian. When coming out of a past with those who are not persons of faith, it is easy to hide your light under a bushel and in so doing, denying your faith and your Savior and what He means to you.

> Never agree to do something in order to impress people or because you fear what they may think or say about it if you don't.[23] (Joyce Meyer)

4. Peter's courage to overcome prejudice.

God used Peter in a miraculous way to open the door to Gentiles to receive the gospel. It happened this way. Peter is given a dream supernaturally from God. In it he saw heaven open and a huge sheet comes down, picturing all kinds of animals, reptiles, and birds. A voice says, "Peter, kill and eat." This was something not done in the Jewish culture. Three times the voice said kill and eat then the sheet was taken back up to heaven. Peter said, "Lord, I can't do that." (Acts 10:11-14) You may be used to being thought of as unclean as Peter did about those unclean animals. Some Jews likened Gentiles sinners to the unclean animals and distanced themselves from them. People may have thought you unredeemable. Many would never choose to eat with you. But you can carry this same attitude with certain people who you think are also unredeemable: maybe very rich people, people of a certain race, or culture or religion. Even in the drug culture, there can be class prejudices in which you think better of yourself than a certain kind of user unlike you.

At about the same time, Peter has visitors from the house of Cornelius, a Roman centurion inviting Peter to his house. This is something Peter had never done or would ever do except, this time the Holy Spirit instructed Peter to go, and so he went. (Acts 10:17-26)

In Acts 10:27 Peter journeyed to Caesarea and entered Cornelius' house and it was one small step for this Jewish disciple, but one giant step for world evangelism! The Holy Spirit poured out His grace on those Gentiles, proving God is no respecter of persons. Peter, in obeying the Holy Spirit, was his way of embracing the principal of Step 10, admitting he was wrong about the Gentiles being shut out from those not of the *circumcision* (those following Jewish traditions).

As we continue to go on, we will continue to see things in us that need changing. It is not as though we need to have a specific time and place to do a personal inventory. As we spend time in prayer and in the Word, we will be sensitive to the Holy Spirit's voice. Today, I got a call from the New York City Department of Correction about an appointment with them. It made me think that there is also a Department of Correction called the Father, Son, and Holy Spirit. Making amends is about "correction."

> Get all the advice and correction you can, so you will be wise the rest of your life. (Proverbs 19:20 NLT)

FOLLOW UP QUESTIONS AND REFLECTIONS ON STEP 10

1. Even in your worst messed-up-living, did you have prejudices towards certain types of people?

2. While taking this 12 Step journey, have you, like Peter, had an, "I'm going fishing" moment, as if to consider whether following Jesus is worth it?

3. If, like Peter, you changed and recommitted yourself to be a true follower of Jesus, describe when and how that happened.

4. Peter had to overcome his past Jewishness to fully embrace the new life in Christ. Have you had to overcome certain religious practices in following Jesus?

5. At any point did your successes in your new life make you prideful?

CONTINUE... INVENTORY

FEEDBACK FROM A PARTICIPANT OF STEP 10

Throughout my transformative journey of discipleship, I endeavor to emulate Christ's actions, constantly evaluating how my decisions, actions, and treatment of others align with His character. When I fall short, I readily admit my wrongdoing and take accountability. Denying responsibility is a detrimental trait often seen in addicts. If I shun responsibility, it serves as a warning sign that I may be regressing into my previous irresponsible ways, believing I am incapable of wrongdoing. This behavior is rooted in pride, the source of all harm, as stated in Proverbs 16:18: "Pride goes before destruction, and a haughty spirit before stumbling."

By cultivating humility, I prevent myself from prioritizing my own interests above others', enabling me to acknowledge and take responsibility for my mistakes. David's story offers a compelling example. Only after wholeheartedly repenting and assuming responsibility for his actions did he experience true transformation. Prior to admitting his wrongs, he resorted to lying, killing, cheating, and deceiving Bathsheba, the people, and those who trusted him. Repentance, both before God and Nathan, laid the foundation for rebuilding his life and restoring broken relationships. I find this example inspiring, guiding me to seek God's forgiveness when I err, and to openly acknowledge my mistakes to myself and others. —Ray Rosa

A PRAYER TO PRAY IN STEP 10

"Surely Lord, knowing You are with me encourages my heart and helps me to continue forward. You work all things together for my edification, and even the trials I experience are for my good and Your glory. Your precious Word gives me assurance, directs me through the changing seasons of life, and reminds me that no matter what I face, I can do so with absolute confidence. You have delivered me through many trials and will continue to do so. You have set me free from bondage and persistently work in me so I can walk in Your liberty. Your loving, faithful presence will be with me today and will accompany me in all my tomorrows." (Charles Stanley)

11
PRAYING... FOR HIS WILL

Step 11: Sought through prayer and meditation to improve our conscious contact with God *as we understood Him*, praying only for knowledge of His will for us and the power to carry it out.

Oh, the joys of those who do not follow the advice of the wicked, or stand around with sinners, or join with mockers. But they delight in the law of the Lord, meditating on it day and night. They are like trees planted along the river bank, bearing fruit each season. Their leaves never wither, and they prosper in all they do. (Psalm 1:1-3 MSG)

> You may forget that at every moment you are entirely dependent on God.[24] (C.S. Lewis)

You have reached a point of immense achievement—of course with God's help. Hopefully your journey (spiritually, emotionally, and naturally) is a time of blessing and peace. Your new normal replaces the old abnormal and your hopelessness has been left in the shadows of having now a lively and living hope—all because you allowed God into the abyss of your troublesome past and rebuilt your life on a new foundation of the knowledge of God together with a commitment to do His will.

Before looking at a Bible hero who lived out the meaning of Step 11, let's review where you have come from:

- Steps 1-3 were, "I admit I have a problem and need to change."

- Steps 4-9: You took the engine of your soul to God's Repair Shop for a Tune Up, Holy Oil Change, and New Tire treads to keep you road worthy, and when you admitted to the list of personal behavior changes needed you said, "Yes, Yes Lord," and again, "Yes."

- Step 10 is a time to look again to see if when taking yet another personal inventory, it provided new perceived wrongs that need to be made right.

Step 11 is living out a God-Planned Life as a life-commitment in everyday life to following God's Way, God's Truth, and God's Life (John 14:6). It's about the journey of faith rather than just step-by-step moments. This is a Step-

Up to living in constant contact with God daily through prayer, the reading of God's Word, and maintaining strong spiritual relationship with others (including those who may have a past like yours, but also those who have a strong and mature walk with God.)

So now, are you ready to embrace a new "high," a life lived without liquid poisons, powder pain killers and similar kind of daily dependencies? Are you ready for keeping the Main Thing the Main Thing according to the Bible and what you have learned about your Higher Power in Jesus Christ? Are you willing to accept the discipline, commitment, and challenges of replacing your will, your "won't", and your 'I can't do it" attitude with "I can do all things through Christ who strengthens me." (Philippians 3:13)

> Relying on God has to begin all over again every day as if nothing had yet been done.[25] (C.S. Lewis)

There are various Bible characters who exemplify perseverance in all of life's challenges. One was Caleb who for 45 years remained faithful among a nation of unfaithful people. There was Ruth, who followed a divine leading into

Israel as a foreigner to serve Jehovah God. Esther risked her life to save the Jews from a holocaust. Of course, Jesus, the Apostle Paul, and Jesus' twelve disciples are examples of perseverance and faithfulness. To persevere in walking out the lessons learned, it requires making Step 11 a daily practice. One man who did this was the disciple named Thomas (Doubting Thomas), so named by John the writer of the Fourth Gospel. We can learn three important things about him as a testimony of Step 11.

1. He improved his contact with God.

This meant going to Bethany near Jerusalem with Jesus when Lazarus had died. At that time being anywhere near Jerusalem was potentially dangerous for Jesus, and it would have also been for His disciples. Thomas speaks up saying, "Let us also go, that we may die with Him." (John 11:16) Was this a statement of doubt? (After all Thomas was known as the *doubting one* among the disciples.) I think not! It was a bold statement of identification with Jesus—a willingness to follow Jesus all the way even to death, if necessary. Many of the disciples eventually did, including Thomas who died much later a martyr.

In Step 11 the meaning "to improve our consciousness of God" means to accept the path He takes us on, even if it means facing the trials and tests that go along in following that path. Remember after the resurrection, Peter was with some of the disciples and Thomas was among them. Peter said, "I am going fishing." Thomas went along with this seemingly detour off the path of following Jesus. Yet, I wonder if in his heart he questioned whether this was the "Way," the path they should be taking.

Once you decide to follow Jesus, you should as Step 11 says, "Praying for the knowledge of His will for us and the power to carry it out." Doing Step 11 is a milestone Step. It is a commitment of exchanging your will of doing things to God's will no matter what that may be. It is not easy facing those who knew you once as a failure. They may not be forgiving, patient, or understanding. Keep God's will as your focus, your faith, and the path to follow regardless of how tough it gets. You've heard of "tough love," what is given to others. Give yourself *tough love* by being strong during hard times.

2. Thomas knew the Way and the will of God, for he had asked the Lord to show him.

Thomas had heard Jesus clearly say to him, "I am the way." It was said in the context of Jesus telling His disciples that he was going to be leaving them. Thomas responded: "Lord, we do not know where You are going, and how can we know the way?" (John 14:3-5) It was Thomas saying, *"Lord. If You're leaving us, where does that leave us? How can we know the way when You're gone?* You may wonder the same thing: *"How can I know the way after completing all the Steps?"* This is why it's important to practice daily prayer and meditating on God's Word. Through prayer we speak to God and through the Scriptures He will speak to us. Psalm 1 speaks of meditating on the Law day and night. I wrote on this verse in my *Challenge Study Bible* the following:

MEDITATE OR MEDICATE. It only takes changing one letter to make a difference between a sound mind and a possibly damaged mind: meditate or medicate. If the mind meditates on the Word of God and delights in it day and night, there will be evidence of fruitful character in that person's life.

3. Take your doubts to the Lord and they can turn into a personal revelation of Christ.

Thomas had made a bold statement about doubting Jesus' death and resurrection, saying, "Unless I see in His hands the print of the nails, and put my hand into His side, I will not believe." (John 20:25) With that declaration, "I will not believe" Thomas earned the title of Doubting Thomas.

> Then He [Jesus] said to Thomas, "Reach your finger here, and look at My hands; and reach your hand here, and put it in My side. Do not be unbelieving, but believing." And Thomas answered and said to Him, "My Lord and my God." (John 20:27-28) (This is one of the most powerful declarations of the deity of Christ in the Bible.)

It has been said we must enter the vestibule of doubt on the way to the sanctuary of faith. This certainly was the case with Thomas.

When Jesus came to His disciples in John 20:26, the Scripture says, "And after eight days His disciples" were in a room where Jesus appeared to them and Jesus told Thomas to see and feel the evidence of His crucifixion and thus His resurrection proof. The disciples could see with their own eyes and Thomas by his touch the evidence of the cross—it so happened eight days after the resurrection. Nothing is trivial in the Bible. Ray Comfort in his *Evidence Bible* writes about a scientific fact in the Bible that took place eight days after His resurrection. Comfort writes:

> Babies are circumcised on the eighth day because this is the day the coagulating factor in the blood, *called prothrombin,* is the highest. Medical science has discovered that this is when the human body's immune system is at its peak. Just as the eighth day was the God-given timing for circumcision (Gen. 17:12), there is a God-given timing for every person who is circumcised with the circumcision made without hands" (Col. 2:11). Jesus appeared to Thomas on the eighth day. What Thomas saw cut away the flesh of his unbelieving heart. He became a Jew inwardly as his circumcision became "that of the heart, in the Spirit, not in the letter." (Romans 2:11)[26]

FOLLOW UP QUESTIONS AND REFLECTIONS ON STEP 11

1. What was your biggest doubt as you began the 12 Steps?

2. What is there about Thomas that helped you gain some insight about yourself?

3. In what way or ways has your will conflicted with God's will?

4. During moments of doubt what did you (or do you) need, of some proof from the Lord to help you overcome those doubts?

5. As you look to the future, what is your biggest fear?

FEEDBACK FROM A PARTICIPANT OF STEP 11

Through the pages of the Bible, I unearth unwavering strength for life's journey, solace during trying times, a beacon of hope in moments of despair, and tranquility amid life's tempests. In our human existence, we traverse a spectrum of emotions and encounters that may entice us to stray from God's path. Many erroneously assume that refraining from alcohol or drugs suffices to guarantee well-being. In my personal experience, I've discovered that the adversary won't necessarily employ alcohol or drugs as his primary temptations. Rather, he cunningly employs subtle influences that, if conceded, could eventually lead me back to the pit of addiction. It's these inconspicuous triggers that warrant my vigilance. My safeguard lies in my unwavering pursuit of the Lord and His divine purpose for my life. While apprehension of regression or relapse doesn't grip me, I strive to approach life with a profound reverence for God and the sacrificial act He undertook on the cross for my sake. I endeavor to live each day in devotion to Him, aligning my actions with His will, and actively contributing to positive transformation within my sphere of influence. The catalyst for catalyzing change in others emerges not from my personal efforts alone, but from the empowering presence of the Holy Spirit, a power reinforced through my dialogues with God in prayer and my immersion in His word. —Ray Rosa

A SHORT PRAYER TO PRAY

"Lord, You said, 'Do not fear, for I am with you; do not be dismayed, for I am your God. I will strengthen you and help you; I will uphold you with my righteous right hand.' Thank you for this promise saying, 'I am the Lord God who takes you by your right hand' and you are saying to me 'Do not fear; I will help you.' (Isaiah 41:10, 13) By faith, I pray this prayer now. Also Lord, I want to do Your will above all and not to fall back into doing my will or what others want me to do if it is not Your will."

A PROMISE OF GOD

Yet I will rejoice in the Lord! I will be joyful in the God of my salvation! The sovereign Lord is my strength! He makes me surefooted as a deer, able to tread upon the heights.

(Habakkuk 3:18-19 NLT)

12

CARRY... THIS MESSAGE

STEP 12: Having had a spiritual awakening as the result of these steps, we tried to carry this message to others and to practice these principles in all our affairs.

Live wisely among those who are not believers, and make the most of the opportunity. Let your conversation be gracious and attractive so that you have the right response for everyone. (Colossians 4:5-6 NLT)

Let your light shine before men, that they may see your good works and glorify your Father in heaven. (Matthew 5:16)

> We are mirrors whose brightness is wholly derived from the sun that shines on us.[27] (C.S. Lewis)

Never forget what it was like for you when first taking the Big Step to do the 12 Step process. You may have entered it just to "check it out" and maybe not intending to go as far as you have. But here you are now, doing the last step which in reality is a Step Up into a new place and experience for you—sharing what you know and have learned over the recent past with others. If for sure and in truth you are on a new path, a path that C.S. Lewis quotes about, you are a mirror reflecting "the sun that shines" on you. I would add it is also a reflection of the Son of God that shines in you and through you.

It's like "show and tell" time, but different than when in school you were given the assignment to choose something to talk about, showing something that represented what you were going to "tell" your fellow students. In this case, as an adult and a potential 12 Step graduate, it is *telling* about your newfound path by *showing* that you are living what you want to tell others. As this Step says, "Practice these principals in all our affairs." Our *telling* others about your "spiritual awakening" needs to be proceeded by living out in practice the new life God has given you.

"Talk is cheap" as the saying goes, and there is nothing that cheapens God's grace more than when you don't back up what you tell by the way you live. If you don't live the talk, you're a hypocrite and an imposter. Don't be a bad advertisement for the 12 Steps or for The Higher Power. If your walk backs up your talk, you have the opportunity to find a new purpose for your life—pointing others to the way of hope out of hopelessness. This will be a new and wonderful experience for you. Instead of being an example of failure, you can be an example of success. But stay humble in doing so. Stay connected to others who are and have walked out the 12 Steps.

> Follow God's example, as dearly loved children, and walk in the way of love, just as Christ loved us... (Ephesians 5:1-2 NIV)

As you try to help newcomers, be careful that you don't get impatient with them. Be patient. After all, they are a reflection of what you once were, and remember others were patient and longsuffering with you on your journey of faith. Like any newborn, they first take small steps before being able to take larger ones. It's the same when it comes to the new birth in Christ.

As you have opportunity to "carry this message to others" you will gain strength and purpose in working out your newfound faith and freedom. The Bible character I'd like you to get to know is Philip, Philip Number Two, that is.

It's easy to get confused over the fact the Bible mentions two Philips. One was an apostle and the other was the evangelist mentioned in the book of Acts. The most well-known Philip was one of the twelve original disciples who followed Jesus.

In certain ways, both "Philips" are examples of wanting to bring others to faith in The Higher Power. Philip Number One was the only disciple that Jesus sought out to ask him to be one of His followers. John 1:43 says, "The following day Jesus wanted to go to Galilee, and He found Philip and said to him, 'Follow Me.'" Then immediately this Philip sought to bring others to Christ by going to Nathanael his friend saying to him, "We have found Him—Jesus of Nazareth, the son of Joseph." (John 1:45)

Philip Number Two was a deacon in the church, chosen because he was "full of faith and the Holy Spirit" to be a part of food distribution to the widows who were in the newly formed, early church. However, he felt a call to preach the Word wherever he could. There are those I define as having the call as an Evangelist with a capitol "E" and others as an evangelist with a small "e". The former are like Billy Graham preaching to thousands in stadiums and arenas; or like my late mother Ann Wilkerson who never missed an opportunity for a one-on-one talk with someone about Jesus.

After the stoning of Stephen recorded in Acts 7:54-59, great persecution was experienced by the New Testament church and many were scattered throughout Judea and Samaria. "Philip (Number Two) went down to Samaria and proclaimed the Messiah there." (Acts 8:4-8) Here are some lessons to be learned from the Philip Number Two:

1. People in crisis situations are most open to the gospel.

Perhaps it was the crisis of addiction that caused you to seek help. If possible, seek out others in places where it is safe for you to encounter those who need help. With sensitivity, compassion, and truthfulness share what God has done for you. Because of your past, you probably can recognize the signs of someone on a downward spiral. Purposely cross their path to point them to where they can take steps to sobriety and salvation.

Philip was sent to an out of the way place where the Holy Spirit had prepared a spiritually hungry foreigner who as a result of visiting Jerusalem, became curious about their religion and obtained a copy of the book of Isaiah. (See Acts 8:26-40) You never know where and when you might have a divine encounter with a seeker after truth. There are always those who are candidates for salvation, even when they don't know this until someone tells and shows them.

2. Look and listen to what may be God's voice telling you to go to a certain place where you might encounter a person who needs help.

This Philip heard the angel of the Lord saying, "Go down the desert road that goes down from Jerusalem to Gaza." (Acts 8:26) On that road was the very man that needed answers for his spiritual hunger.

Now, I'm sure you're saying, "Yeah! Like I'm going to have an angel of the Lord speak to me?" Wait just a minute. Have you ever heard of an "angel unaware?" (Hebrews 13:1-2 NIV) That is when God can use a messenger (naturally or supernaturally) to guide you to someone who is hungry to know God and find freedom from their bondage. You could feel led to talk to a neighbor or a co-worker who they themselves need help or they have a loved one who does. People can cross your path that are sent your way by the Holy Spirit. It can happen naturally and supernaturally.

3. When wanting to "carry the message to others" there are times when the opportunity of a lifetime must be seized in the lifetime of the opportunity.

This was the case with Philip Number Two. It so happened a man of great importance representing the Queen of the Ethiopians had just left Jerusalem where he had gone to worship. "On his way home he was sitting in his chariot reading the book of Isaiah, the prophet. The Spirit told Philip, 'Go to the chariot and stay near it.'" (Acts 8:29) The end story is that Philip was at the right place at the right time to answer this man's questions. The result is that he asked to be baptized in water as a sign of his conversion. As he came up out of the water, Philip was gone (apparently supernaturally) and the man, a eunuch, "went on his way rejoicing." (Acts 8:30-39 NIV) What if Philip had not obeyed the Spirit's calling? What if he had not explained and interpreted the question of this influential man who went back to his country, his people, and his Queen as a newborn believer in Jesus, the Messiah? The Queen was a God-fearing Gentile who worshiped the Jewish God, and when the Government Treasurer (who was the man in the chariot) went back to her kingdom, I'm sure it strengthened her faith, resulting in more coming to faith in that foreign land.

Yes, the opportunity of a lifetime often comes only once and needs taken advantage of. Prior to this, Philip was as an itinerate evangelist going to Samaria "and proclaimed the Messiah there." (Acts 8:4-8) As a result of that visit, many were healed, "so there was great joy in that city."

4. **Apparently, this Philip recognized his calling was to preach the gospel in other towns until he reached Caesarea, his hometown.**

Some 20 years later Paul visits Philip and his four virgin daughters who prophesied. (Acts 21:8-9) The fact that Paul visited Philip and that he had four daughters that were used with the gift of prophecy shows this was a man who is an example of "show and tell." His daughters followed in their father's footsteps and also became evangelists. He showed by the faithfulness of his life the reality of a proven faith and witness thereof of his faith. May we all do the same.

FEEDBACK FROM PARTICIPANT OF STEP 12

I would say that, yes, I had a spiritual awakening, but I also had an encounter with Christ. Anyone can be awakened spiritually. There's meditation, yoga, chanting, lighting incense and many other things that claim to awaken people spiritually. However, my experience was one of a crisis that led to a need that then led to an encounter. The crisis being what I was going through emotionally and even spiritually. These things I was unaware of. This crisis led me to seek refuge and healing in drugs and alcohol, amongst other things. My need was to medicate the pains I did not know existed. However, the real need was that of being saved. That need for salvation is what led to my encounter with Christ. The encounter with Christ therefore spiritually awakened me. His touching my life instantly healed me of addiction, not necessarily of all of the emotional things. Those He is still working on in what I understand to be the discipleship process. However, this awakening and encounter provoked me to share my experience with others, including those who are still in addiction. It's the woman at the well experience. She has an encounter with Christ at the well, but when He speaks to her heart and pain, she is awakened! She then runs to her city to proclaim all that Christ has spoken about her, meaning all he knew about her heart. She knew that because Christ pointed these things out about her life that He was the Messiah, because only He could do that. That revelation caused her to evangelize her city. That encounter caused her to preach to those whom she had used to medicate herself, like the men of the city.

The opposite can be said of the ten lepers that Jesus healed, that only one had a spiritual encounter and awakening. This sharing with others is what I call witnessing. When I practice this, it reminds me of where I came from, what Christ healed me of, and what He can do for others, if they surrender to him. —Ray Rosa

FOLLOW UP QUESTIONS AND REFLECTIONS ON STEP 12

1. When sharing your story of sobriety with others, how do you think it will help you?

2. Are you more a people-person or a loner. If needed, how might you overcome the latter?

3. Why is practicing these principles in your life while carrying the message to other so important?

4. Galatians 6:1 says, "If someone is caught in a sin, help restore the person." But the verse also says in this process to "watch yourself, or you may be tempted." What does this verse mean to you?

5. Think about when you were still in your old lifestyle. Did someone carry the message of their "spiritual awakening" to you? As you recall that, how might it help you now in doing the same?

A PRAYER TO PRAY

"Lord, help me to be Your instrument of praise and purpose to show others the way to You. I want others to experience this new way of life You've given me. Help me to be bold for You, unashamed of who You are by sharing my testimony, and help me be patient with those who have not yet taken the steps I've taken. Give me strength to not give up on others who reject You. Lead me to those who need what You have given me. Lead others to me, as well. Lord, my desire now is to make a normal part of my life being Christlike, being loving and kind, and to the best that I can to be faithful and obedient in doing Your will. Amen!"

A PROMISE OF GOD

And now to Him who can keep you on your feet, standing tall in His bright presence, fresh and celebrating—to our one God, our only Savior, through Jesus Christ, our Master, be glory, majesty, strength, and rule before all time, and now, and to the end of all time. Yes!

(Jude 1:24-25 MSG)

OTHER RECOMMENDED RESOURCE MATERIAL FOR 12 STEP PARTICIPANTS

1. THE CHALLENGE STUDY BIBLE

Especially written commentary for those in recovery, but not exclusively for such persons. The commentary is also for the general reader and for Bible Study.

2. THE FIRST STEP TO FREEDOM

An excellent companion source to participants of *12 Steps Through the Bible*. Prayer is essential in seeking control of a life-controlling problem and this book outlines the practical and scriptural importance of prayer as a First Step to sobriety, sanity, and salvation.

3. 29:11 THE JEREMIAH CODE

This book unwraps the meaning of the famous Bible verse of Jeremiah 29:11, intended to address relapse prevention as well as God's wonderful promise of restoration for relapsers.

4. A DRINK CALLED JOY
A SUPERNATURAL ANSWER TO ADDICTION

This book shows how Joy trumps all other sources of happiness like drugs or alcohol.

5. KEPT FROM FALLING

A recommended resource as a follow-up to finishers of *12 Steps Through the Bible*. It contains 7 lessons on how to maintain recovery and how to be one of the "Recovered."

All the above books available through Amazon.

If you want to share feedback with Don Wilkerson you can do so at dwilker@aol.com.

ABOUT THE AUTHOR

Donald W. Wilkerson is the fifth child of Kenneth and Ann Wilkerson. He was born in Cambria County, Pennsylvania into an Assembly of God pastor's home. Don, the name he goes by, was given the middle name Wesley, after Charles Wesley. With that name Don contends he was destined to become a preacher. The Wilkerson family lived in North Cambria (originally Barnesboro), then moved to the Pittsburgh area for ten years where Don, in addition to being called to the ministry there, he also became a Pittsburg Pirate and Steeler fan.

In the mid 1950's, they moved to Scranton to a church where Don, at the age of sixteen, first began to preach. From there he want to Eastern Bible Institute in Pennsylvania. There he met Cynthia Hudson from Plainfield, Vermont and they got married in 1961. Don had already at that point been asked by his brother David to join him in New York City to work in a new street outreach to gangs called Teen Challenge. Don and Cindy moved into the first residential discipleship-rehab home at 416 Clinton Avenue Brooklyn where, from then until now, thousands of gang members and drug addicts have found new life in a program founded on 2 Corinthians

ABOUT THE AUTHOR

5:17, "If any man be in Christ Jesus, old things pass away; behold, all things become new."

Don is noted for developing the first faith-based, Christ-centered program at what has become the Flagship Center, now spread around the world. In the mid 1980's Don joined his brother in founding Times Square Church where for nine years Don was one of the preaching pastors. In 1995, Don then founded Global Teen Challenge, travelling the world helping to open Teen Challenge Centers in numerous countries. Don and Cindy retired to their home in Central Virginia in 2007 where he began a new ministry writing books and materials for faith-based leaders and discipleship material for students in the program.

Don and Cindy interrupted retirement for a period to return to the Brooklyn Center for a more than expected long season in 2008 and then re-retied to go back to his vocation of writing. 12 Steps Through the Bible is the fifteenth book he has written. Don and Cindy have three adult children and five grandchildren. Don also now is helping some faith-based ministries to operate Thrift Stores as a means of raising funds for the program, helping to secure gifts-in-kind to sale in those stores.

ENDNOTES

[1] Friends in Recovery, *The Twelve Steps for Christians* (Boise: RPI Publishing, Inc., 1994), Kindle.
[2] Beth Moore, *Daniel - Bible Study Book: Lives of Integrity, Words of Prophecy* (Brentwood: Lifeway Press, 2006)
[3] Max Lucado, *When Christ Comes* (Nashville: Thomas Nelson, 2014).
[4] C.S. Lewis, *God in the Dock* (New York, HarperCollins, 2014), Kindle.
[5] Don Wilkerson, *The Challenge Study Bible* (Newberry: Bridge-Logos Inc., 2019)
[6] Tony Evans, *God Is Up to Something Great* (New York: The Crown Publishing Group, 2011), Kindle.
[7] John Calvin, *The Institutes of the Christian Religion* (2010), Kindle.
[8] Sheila Walsh, *It's Okay Not to Be Okay* (Ada: Baker Publishing Group, 2018), Kindle.
[9] Friends in Recovery, *The Twelve Steps for Christians* (Boise: RPI Publishing, Inc., 1994), Kindle.
[10] Beth Moore, *Daniel - Bible Study Book: Lives of Integrity, Words of Prophecy* (Brentwood: Lifeway Press, 2006)
[11] Franklin Graham; Ross Rhodes, *All for Jesus: A Devotional* (New York: HarperCollins Christian Publishing, 2008), Kindle.
[12] David Wilkerson, *Revival on Broadway!: Messages to God's Church from the Heart of Times Square* (Wilkerson Trust Publications, 1996)
[13] https://www.aacle.org/twelve-step-prayers/ (Fourth Step Prayer)
[14] Dwight Lyman Moody, *Weighed and Wanting, Addresses on the Ten Commandments* (2011), Kindle.
[15] Friends in Recovery, *The Twelve Steps for Christians* (Boise: RPI Publishing, Inc., 1994), Kindle.
[16] Henry Cloud; John Townsend, *Safe People* (Grand Rapids: Zondervan, 2009), Kindle.
[17] Saint Augustine, Bishop of Hippo, *Confessions* (Illustrated, 2014), Kindle.
[18] Jim Cymbala, *You Were Made for More* (Grand Rapids: Zondervan, 2014), Kindle.
[19] Friends in Recovery, *The Twelve Steps for Christians* (Boise: RPI Publishing, Inc., 1994), Kindle.
[20] Ibid.
[21] Ibid.
[22] C.S. Lewis, *Mere Christianity* (New York, HarperCollins, 2009), Kindle.
[23] Joyce Meyer, *Wake Up to the Word* (New York: FaithWords, 2106), Kindle.
[24] C.S. Lewis, *Mere Christianity* (New York, HarperCollins, 2009), Kindle.
[25] C.S. Lewis, *Letters to an American Lady* (New York: HarperCollins, 2014), Kindle.
[26] Ray Comfort, *The Evidence Study Bible* (Newberry: Bridge-Logos Inc., 2019), Kindle.
[27] C.S. Lewis, *The Four Loves* (New York: HarperCollins, 2017), Kindle.